WASHINGTON & OREGON

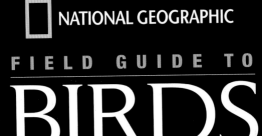

NATIONAL GEOGRAPHIC

FIELD GUIDE TO

BIRDS

D0824271

WASHINGTON & OREGON

NATIONAL GEOGRAPHIC

FIELD GUIDE TO

BIRDS

Edited by JONATHAN ALDERFER

National Geographic
Washington, D.C.

INTRODUCTION

If you want to see birds under good conditions, go to National Wildlife Refuges (NWRs), state wildlife areas and habitat-diverse coastal bays. The best areas in eastern Oregon include Malheur NWR, Summer Lake, the Klamath Basin, Wallowa County in winter and McNary Dam.

On the coast, Coos Bay is a great birding area, especially outer coast sites. Yaquina Bay is exceptionally birdy, as are Tillamook Bay and the south jetty of the Columbia River.

Interior western Oregon offers excellent birding at Fern Ridge Reservoir, Finley, Ankeny and Baskett Slough NWRs, Sauvie Island and wetlands west of Portland, Jackson Bottoms and Fernhill being among the best. In Portland, Eastmoreland Park supports a wide variety of waterfowl.

From temperate rainforest to shrub-steppe, every corner of Washington offers worthwhile birding. Washington has many NWRs and other birding sites just waiting for you to explore. Two National Parks, Olympic and Mount Rainier, provide access to high elevation birds. The coast offers some of the finest birding, especially at Cape Flattery and Grays Harbor.

Juanita Bay Park in Kirkland and Montlake Fill in Seattle offer good birding in urban areas. Nisqually NWR and Ridge-field NWR are fantastic places to see a huge selection of birds. The Skagit and Samish Flats are famous for raptors but also provide exceptional winter birding for waterfowl and sparrows.

Birders find specialty birds in ponderosa pine forests in the Wenas area. Turnbull NWR near Cheney is rich in waterfowl. Potholes Reservoir includes a colony of herons and egrets. The Walla Walla River Delta is one of several spots where you can view shorebirds.

We dedicate our work on this book to the memory of young birders gone before their time, Jason Starfire and Ryan Beaulieu.

ALAN CONTRERAS
Co-editor, *Birds of Oregon*

CONTENTS

SELECTED BIRDING SITES OF
WASHINGTON AND OREGON

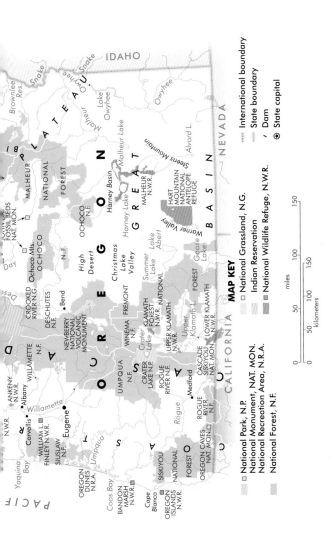

IDAHO

Snake

Owyhee

Brownlee Res.

Malheur

Lake Owyhee

Owyhee

B I

PLATEAU

MALHEUR

NATIONAL

JOHN DAY FOSSIL BEDS NAT. MON.

Harney Basin

Malheur Lake

FOREST

Day

Alvord L.

Ochoco Mts.

OCHOCO

G R E A T

MALHEUR N.W.R.

Steens Mountain

N.F.

OCHOCO N.F.

CROOKED RIVER N.G.

High Desert

Christmas Lake Valley

Warner Valley

HART MOUNTAIN NATIONAL ANTELOPE REFUGE

B A S I N

Bend

DESCHUTES N.F.

NEWBERRY NATIONAL VOLCANIC MONUMENT

O R E G O N

NEVADA

WILLAMETTE

N.F.

FREMONT

Summer Lake

Lake Abert

UMPQUA N.F.

WINEMA N.F.

Crater Lake

Lake

FOREST

Goose Lake

ANKENY N.W.R.

Albany

CRATER LAKE N.P.

KLAMATH FOREST N.W.R.

UPPER KLAMATH NATIONAL

CALIFORNIA

Willamette

Corvallis

WILLIAM L. FINLEY N.W.R.

Eugene

ROGUE RIVER N.F.

Upper Klamath L.

UPPER KLAMATH N.W.R.

MAP KEY

SIUSLAW N.F.

Medford

CASCADE SISKIYOU NAT. MON.

LOWER KLAMATH N.W.R.

Rogue

Umpqua

ROGUE RIVER N.F.

Yaquina Bay

OREGON DUNES N.R.A.

BANDON MARSH N.W.R.

Cape Blanco

SISKIYOU

NATIONAL

FOREST

OREGON CAVES NAT. MON.

OREGON ISLANDS N.W.R.

Coos Bay

P A C I F

- - - - International boundary
· · · · · State boundary
⁄ Dam
⊛ State capital

National Grassland, N.G.
Indian Reservation
National Wildlife Refuge, N.W.R.

National Park, N.P.
National Monument, NAT. MON.
National Recreation Area, N.R.A.
National Forest, N.F.

miles
0   50   100   150

kilometers
0   50   100   150

LOOKING AT BIRDS

What do the artist and the nature lover share? A passion for being attuned to the world and all of its complexity, via the senses. Every time you go out into the natural world, or even view it through a window, you have another opportunity to see what is there. And the more you know what you are looking at, the more you see.

Even if you are not yet a committed birder, it makes sense to take a field guide with you when you go out for a walk or a hike. Looking for and identifying birds will sharpen and heighten your perceptions, and intensify your experience. And you'll find that you notice everything else more acutely—the terrain, the season, the weather, the plant life, other animal life.

Birds are beautiful, complex animals that live everywhere around us in our towns and cities, and in distant places we dream of visiting. Here in North America more than 900 species have been recorded—from abundant commoners to the rare and exotic. A comprehensive field reference like the *National Geographic Field Guide to the Birds of North America* is essential for understanding that big picture. If you are taking a spring walk in the Washington/Oregon countryside, however, you may want something simpler: a guide to the birds you are most likely to see, which slips easily into a pocket.

This guide is designed to provide an introduction to the common birds—and a few rare birds—you might encounter in Washington and Oregon: how to identify them, how they behave, and where to find them, with specific locations.

Discovery, observation, and identification of birds can be exciting, whether you are a novice or expert. As an artist and birder for most of my life, I know that every time I go out to look at birds, I see more clearly and have a greater appreciation for the natural world around me and my own place in it.

JONATHAN ALDERFER
Editor

National Geographic Field Guide to Birds: Washington & Oregon is designed to help beginning and practiced birders alike identify birds in the field and introduce them to the region's varied birdlife. The book is organized by bird families, following the order in the *Check-list to the Birds of North America,* by the American Ornithologists' Union. Families share structural characteristics, and by learning these shared characteristics early, birders can establish a basis for a lifetime of identifying birds and related family members with great accuracy—sometimes merely at a glance. (For quick reference in the field, use the color and alphabetical indexes at the back of this book.)

A family may have one member or dozens of members, or species. In this book each family is identified by its common name in English along the right-hand border of each spread. Each species is also identified in English, with its Latin genus and species—its scientific name—found directly underneath. One species is featured in each entry.

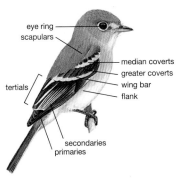

eye ring
scapulars
median coverts
greater coverts
wing bar
flank
tertials
secondaries
primaries

Least Flycatcher

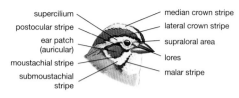

Lark Sparrow

supercilium
postocular stripe
ear patch
(auricular)
moustachial stripe
submoustachial
stripe

median crown stripe
lateral crown stripe
supraloral area
lores
malar stripe

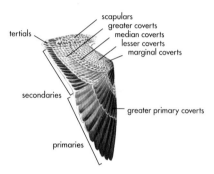

Great Black-backed Gull, upper wing

tertials
scapulars
greater coverts
median coverts
lesser coverts
marginal coverts
secondaries
greater primary coverts
primaries

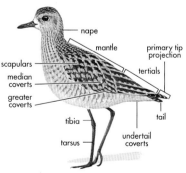

Pacific Golden-Plover

nape
mantle
primary tip
projection
scapulars
tertials
median
coverts
greater
coverts
tibia
tarsus
undertail
coverts
tail

An entry begins with **Field Marks**, the physical clues used to quickly identify a bird, such as body shape and size, bill length, and plumage color or pattern. A bird's body parts yield vital clues to identification, so a birder needs to become familiar with them early on. After the first glance at body type, take note of the head shape and markings, such as stripes, eye rings, and crown markings. Bill shape and color are important as well. Note body and wing details: wing bars, color and pattern of wing feathers at rest, and shape and markings when extended in flight. Tail shape, length, color, and banding may play a big part, too. At left are diagrams detailing the various parts of a bird—its topography—labeled with the term likely to be found in the text of this book.

The main body of each entry is divided into three categories: Behavior, Habitat, and Local Sites. The **Behavior** section details certain characteristics to look or listen for in the field. Often a bird's behavioral characteristics are very closely related to its body type and field marks, such as in the case of woodpeckers, whose chisel-shaped bills, stiff tails, strong legs, and sharp claws enable them to spend most of their lives in an upright position, braced against a tree trunk. The **Habitat** section describes areas that are most likely to support the featured species. Preferred nesting locations of breeding birds are also included in many cases. The **Local Sites** section recommends specific refuges or parks where the featured bird is likely to be found. A section called **Field Notes** finishes each entry, and includes information such as plumage variations within a species; or it may introduce another species with which the featured bird is frequently confused. In either case, an additional drawing may be included to aid in identification.

Finally, a caption underneath each of the photographs gives the season of the plumage pictured, as well as the age and gender of the bird, if discernable. A key to using this informative guide and its range maps follows on the next two pages.

The following numbered callouts point to elements of the sample page spread:

❶ ❷ ❸ ❹ ❺ ❻ ❼ ❽ ❾ ❿

On the spread illustration:

GREEN-WINGED TEAL
Anas crecca L 14" (37 cm)

FIELD MARKS
Male's chestnut head has green ear patch faintly outlined in white
Female has mottled, dusky brown upperparts; white belly and undertail coverts

Behavior
Like other dabbling ducks, feeds at the water's surface or upended, tail in the air and head submerged, to reach aquatic plants, seeds, and snails. The Green-winged teal has a specialized bill for filtering food from the mud. An agile and fast-moving flier, travels in small flocks that synchronize their twists and turns in midair. The Green-winged female emits a high, thrill-like

Habitat
Found on coastal estuaries and tidal marshes, and on shallow lakes and inland ponds, especially those with standing or floating vegetation. Nests are hidden among grasses and weeds, within 200 feet of

Local Sites
Green-winged Teals are widespread in wetland habitats throughout much of Washington and Oregon.

FIELD NOTES he Cinnamon Teal, *Anas cyanoptera*, is strictly a spring and summer visitor to marshes, ponds, and lakes of the area. The male (inset: breeding) is easily separated from the Green-winged, but the females can be more difficult to tell apart. In flight, though, both sexes of Cinnamon Teal show a patch of pale blue on the upper wing.

Breeding | Adult male

❶ **Photograph:** Shows bird in habitat. May be female or male, adult or juvenile. Plumage may be breeding, molting, nonbreeding, or year-round.

❷ **Caption:** Defines the featured bird's plumage, age, and sometimes gender, as seen in the picture.

❸ **Heading:** Beneath the common name find the Latin, or scientific, name. Beside it is the bird's length (L), and sometimes its wingspan (WS). Wingspan is given with birds often seen in flight. Female measurements are given if disparate from male.

❹ **Field Marks:** Gives basic facts for field identification: markings, head and bill shape, and body size.

❺ **Band:** Gives the common name of the bird's family.

❻ **Range Map:** Shows year-round range in purple, breeding range in red, winter range in blue. Areas through which species are likely to migrate are shown in green.

❼ **Behavior:** A step beyond **Field Marks,** gives clues to identify a bird by its habits, such as feeding, flight pattern, courtship, nest-building, or songs and calls.

❽ **Habitat:** Reveals the area a species is most likely to inhabit, such as forests, marshes, grasslands, or urban areas. May include preferred nesting sites.

❾ **Local Sites:** Details local spots to look for the given species.

❿ **Field Notes:** A special entry that may give a unique point of identification, compare two species of the same family, compare two species from different families that are easily confused, or focus on a historic or conservation fact.

On each map of Washington and Oregon, range boundaries are drawn where the species ceases to be regularly seen. Nearly every species will be rare at the edges of its range. The sample map shown below explains the colors and symbols used on each map. Ranges continually expand and contract, so the map is a tool, not a rule. Range information is based on actual sightings and therefore depends upon the number of knowledgeable and active birders in each area.

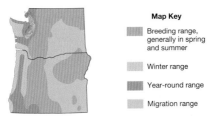

Map Key

Breeding range, generally in spring and summer

Winter range

Year-round range

Migration range

Sample Map: Yellow-rumped Warbler

There are two indexes at the back of this book. The first is a **Color Index** (p. 262), created to help birders quickly find an entry by noting its color in the field. In this index, male birds are labeled by their predominant color: Mostly White, Mostly Black, etc. Note that a bird may have a head of a different color than its label states. That's because its body—the part most noticeable in the field—is the color labeled.

The **Alphabetical Index** (p. 266) is organized by the bird's common name. Next to each entry is a check-off box. Most birders make lists of the birds they see. Some keep several lists, perhaps one of birds in a certain area and another of all the birds they've ever seen—a life list. Such lists enable birders to look back and remember their first sighting of a Downy Woodpecker or an American Kestrel.

Year-round | Adult white morph

SNOW GOOSE

Chen caerulescens L 26" (66 cm) WS 52" (132 cm)

FIELD MARKS
White overall or, less commonly, dark gray-brown; black primaries show in flight

Heavy pinkish bill with black "grinning patch"

Juvenile is dingy gray-brown on head, neck, and upperparts

Behavior
Travels in huge flocks, especially during fall migration. Loud, vocal bird; flocks fly in loose V-formation and long lines, sometimes more than 1,500 miles nonstop, reaching speeds up to 40 mph. Primarily vegetarian, forages on agricultural grains and plants and on all parts of aquatic vegetation. An agile swimmer, commonly rests on water during migration and at wintering grounds. Listen for its harsh, descending *wouk*, heard continuously in flight.

Habitat
Most often seen on grasslands, grainfields, and coastal wetlands, favoring standing shallow freshwater marshes and flooded fields. Breeds in the Arctic.

Local Sites
Winter residents crowd the flooded meadows of the Klamath Basin in Oregon and of the Skagit River Delta in Washington. Large migratory flocks can be seen overhead in spring and fall in broad flyways that traverse the area.

FIELD NOTES Amid a flock of Snow Geese, look as well for the smaller, less common Ross's Goose, *Chen rossii* (inset: white morph). It is set apart by a stubby, triangular bill lacking a "grinning patch" and a shorter neck.

Year-round | Adult "Black" Brant

BRANT

Branta bernicla L 25" (64 cm)

FIELD MARKS

Small, dark, and stocky with black head, neck, breast, and bill

Distinctive whitish patch on each side of neck

White tail coverts conceal black tail in flight

Behavior

Flocks fly low in ragged formation with no evident lead bird. At speeds of up to 60 mph, the Brant is among the fastest and strongest of geese in flight. Feeds during low tide in or near protected coastal bays and estuaries, then takes off for open water once the tide begins to rise. Roosts at night in rafts on open ocean. Call is a low, rolling, throaty *raunk-raunk*.

Habitat

The Brant winters along sea coasts, feeding on the aquatic plants of shallow bays and estuaries, especially eelgrass and sea lettuce. This hardy sea bird is also resilient enough to endure storms on the open ocean, where it roosts at night. Breeds in the Arctic.

Local Sites

Yaquina Bay is a good spot in Oregon to find Brants foraging at low tide. In Washington, look for them in Padilla Bay or at Dungeness National Wildlife Refuge on the Strait of Juan de Fuca.

FIELD NOTES This species is one of the pickiest and least adaptable of North American waterfowl when it comes to its food source, almost exclusively eelgrass or sea lettuce . Therefore its numbers in Washington and Oregon are threatened in coastal bays where eelgrass beds have been reduced by human activity.

Year-round | Adult with chick

CANADA GOOSE

Branta canadensis L 38-45" (97-114 cm) WS 55-60" (140-152 cm)

FIELD MARKS

Black head and neck marked with distinctive white chin strap

In flight, shows large, dark wings, white undertail coverts, and a long protruding neck

Variable gray-brown breast color

Behavior

A common, familiar goose; best known for migrating in large V-formation. Like some other members of its family, the Canada Goose finds a mate and remains monogamous for life. Family groups tend to stay together through the winter. Its distinctive musical call of *honk-a-lonk* makes it easy to identify, even without seeing it. It also makes a murmuring sound when feeding, and a hissing sound when protecting young.

Habitat

Prefers wetlands, grasslands, and cultivated fields within commuting distance of water. It has also adapted successfully to man-made habitats such as golf courses and farms. Female builds nest of sticks, grass, and weeds on dry ground near water.

Local Sites

Canada Geese can be found year-round in wetland habitats throughout much of Washington and Oregon.

FIELD NOTES Ongoing research into the mitochondrial DNA of the Canada Goose has found that the smaller subspecies, such as *hutchinsii* (inset, left), *minima* (inset, center), and *leucopareia* (inset, right) actually belong to their own species, the newly named Cackling Goose, *Branta hutchinsii*.

Year-round | Adult

TUNDRA SWAN

Cygnus columbianus L 52" (132 cm)

FIELD MARKS

White overall with black facial skin

Black, slightly concave bill with yellow spot of variable size in front of eye

Juvenile appears darker with pinkish bill

Behavior

Feeds on aquatic vegetation in shallow water, utilizing its long neck, which enables it to keep its body upright. To take flight, the Tundra Swan runs across water beating its wings. Flies in straight lines or in V-formation, with its neck protruding forward. Following the same routes every year, the Tundra Swan migrates thousands of miles between Arctic breeding grounds and temperate wintering quarters. Call is a noisy, high-pitched bugling or yodeling, often heard at night.

Habitat

Winters in flocks along the coast and considerably inland on shallow ponds, lakes, estuaries, and marshes. Breeds on tundra ponds in Alaska and the Arctic.

Local Sites

Tundra Swans can be found in winter in the Klamath Basin of Oregon or in the Skagit Game Range in Washington, where Trumpeters are known to flock as well.

FIELD NOTES The Trumpeter Swan, *Cygnus buccinator* (inset), is also white overall with a black bill, and visits some of the same winter locales as the Tundra. It is best differentiated by its voice, a single or double honk lower in pitch than the Tundra's, and by its lack of yellow in front of the eyes and a V-shaped forehead. Look for it year-round at Malheur National Wildlife Refuge in Oregon.

Breeding | Adult male

WOOD DUCK

Aix sponsa L 18½" (47 cm)

FIELD MARKS
Male has glossy iridescent head and crest, lined in white; red, white, black, and yellow bill; burgundy breast with white spotting

Female duller overall with large white teardrop-shaped eye patch

Squared-off tail shows in flight

Behavior
Most commonly feeds by picking insects from the water's surface or by tipping into shallows to pluck invertebrates from the bottom, but may also be seen foraging on land. The omnivorous Wood Duck's diet changes throughout the year depending upon available foods and its need for particular proteins or minerals during migration, breeding, and molting. Male Wood Ducks give a soft, upslurred whistle when swimming. Female Wood Ducks have a distinctive rising, squealing flight call of *oo-eek*.

Habitat
Prefers woodlands and forested swamps. Nests in tree cavities or man-made nest boxes.

Local Sites
Wood Ducks can be found year-round in rivers, lakes, and ponds west of the Cascades. In spring, many of them disperse inland to find suitable breeding territory.

FIELD NOTES The Wood Duck female (inset) hatches up to 15 eggs in a single clutch in cavities high up in trees or nest boxes. Once hatched, the young must make a long jump to the water, sometimes 30 feet below. Protected by downy newborn plumage, they generally splash down safely.

Breeding | Adult male

GADWALL

Anas strepera L 20" (51 cm)

FIELD MARKS

Male mostly gray, with a brownish head and back, black tail coverts, and chestnut wing patches

Female mottled brown overall; dark upper mandible has distinctive orange sides

White speculum shows in flight

Behavior
Feeds primarily on aquatic vegetation, insects, and invertebrates in shallow water. Found in pairs or small groups, foraging with its head submerged, but without tipping up like many other dabbling ducks. Also known to dive for its food in deeper waters. Walks well on land, and may be seen foraging in fields or wooded areas for nuts, acorns, and grain. Female's call is a descending series of loud quacks; male sometimes emits a shrill, whistled note.

Habitat
Resides primarily in freshwater habitats, especially those with dense vegetation, but may also be found in some enclosed saltwater habitats. Female builds nest of weeds and grasses on dry land near water.

Local Sites
The Gadwall is widespread year-round throughout the wetlands of Washington and Oregon. Malheur National Wildlife Refuge and Fern Ridge Reservoir are two reliable places to look for this bird in Oregon.

FIELD NOTES The Gadwall can be found in wetland habitats throughout the world. It nests in northern latitudes in Europe, Asia, and North America and winters farther south from India, Africa, and Mexico. Nowhere, though, is it found in abundance—except western North America.

Breeding | Adult male

AMERICAN WIGEON

Anas americana L 19" (48 cm)

FIELD MARKS

White cap and forehead on male; green patch extending back from eyes; white wing patch

Both sexes have large white patch on underwing

Rusty brown chest, flanks, and back; white belly; pointed tail

Behavior
Grazes in fields and was once considered an agricultural pest. Often feeds in shallow water with other duck species; has also been known to forage in deeper waters, and to steal food from diving ducks or coots. Flushes readily if disturbed. Tight flocks careen together impressively. Male's whistle is a three-note *whew-whew-whew;* female gives off a low, harsh quack.

Habitat
Found in various wetland habitats, ranging from marshes to lakes, bays, coastal estuaries, flooded fields, and even golf courses. The American Wigeon's shallow nest is built on dry land among tall weeds.

Local Sites
American Wigeons can be found in winter at a variety of locales west of the Cascades. They nest farther east, especially at sites with dense vegetation such as Malheur National Wildlife Refuge in Oregon.

FIELD NOTES A stray Eurasian Wigeon, *Anas penelope* (inset: breeding male), is actually a regular sight at coastal parks such as Eastmoreland Park in Portland, Oregon, and Green Lake in Seattle, Washington. Usually found amid a flock of American Wigeon, the male is fairly easily distinguished by his reddish brown head and gray flanks.

Breeding | Adult male

MALLARD

Anas platyrhynchos L 23" (58 cm)

FIELD MARKS
Male has metallic green head and
neck, white collar, chestnut breast

Female mottled brown overall;
orange bill marked with black

Both sexes have bright blue
speculum bordered in white; white
tail and underwings

Behavior
A dabbler, the Mallard feeds by tipping into shallows
and plucking seeds, grasses, or invertebrates from the
bottom. Also picks insects from the water's surface.
The courtship ritual of the Mallard consists of the
male pumping his head, dipping his bill, and rearing
up in the water to exaggerate his size. A female signals
consent by duplicating the male's head-pumping.
Listen for the female Mallard's loud, rasping quack.

Habitat
This widespread species occurs wherever shallow fresh
water is to be found, from coastal lagoons to urban
ponds. May be found in winter in some salt marshes
and bays. Nests on the ground in concealing vegetation.

Local Sites
Mallards cope well with man-made habitats and reside
all year in ponds, streams, and city fountains throughout Washington and Oregon.

FIELD NOTES The female Mallard (inset)
is mottled brown overall. Its head is
distinctly grayer than its body, and
it displays a dark eye stripe. Between
June and September, the male resembles
the female, but retains his yellowish bill, while the
female's bill is orange with a dark center.

Breeding | Adult male

NORTHERN SHOVELER

Anas clypeata L 19" (48 cm)

FIELD MARKS
Large spatulate bill

Male has green head, white
breast, chestnut belly; white facial
crescent in fall

Female mottled brown overall,
grayish orange bill

Behavior

This dabbler is equipped with a unique bill that has
comblike bristles to strain plankton and insects from
water. Forages while swimming, its bill submerged or
skimming the surface for aquatic seeds and plants. In
shallow water, the Northern Shoveler sieves through
muddy bottoms for small crustaceans and mollusks.
Listen for the female's deep, descending *whack-whack-
whack-wak-waa,* and during breeding season for the
male's hoarse, unmusical *tuk-tuk-tuk.*

Habitat

Favors small, shallow lakes and ponds, freshwater
and saline marshes, and other smaller bodies of water
densely bordered by emergent vegetation. Nests in
short, dense grasses close to a body of water.

Local Sites

Shovelers are fairly widespread throughout Washington and Oregon, keeping more to the coast in winter,
then dispersing inland to breed. Nisqually National
Wildlife Refuge and other spots along Puget Sound
in Washington host shovelers year-round.

FIELD NOTES Vulnerable to predation by rats, minks, and some
other scavenging mammals, a nesting female shoveler will often
defecate on her eggs to keep them from being eaten.

Breeding | Adult male

NORTHERN PINTAIL

Anas acuta Male L 26" (66 cm) Female L 20" (51 cm)

FIELD MARKS

Male has chocolate brown head; long white neck, breast, and underparts; gray back; long black central tail feathers

Female mottled brown overall

Long neck, slender body, and pointed tail evident in flight

Behavior

Small flocks forage for seeds and aquatic insects in flooded agricultural fields or shallow ponds and marshes. This accomplished flyer is known for spilling out of the sky in a rapid descent and leveling out directly into a landing. In courtship flight, up to half a dozen drakes can be observed pursuing a single hen as she veers and swerves. Male's call is a weak, nasal *geee;* female often utters a gutteral quack.

Habitat

Frequents both freshwater and saltwater marshes, ponds, lakes, and coastal bays. Also found in flooded agricultural fields, especially during winter. Female builds nest in open fields of short grass.

Local Sites

In winter, pintails can be found in a variety of wetlands west of the Cascades. Kent Valley near Puget Sound in Washington is a reliable spot.

FIELD NOTES In winter, coastal bays, such as Yaquina in Oregon and Padilla in Washington, host the Long-tailed Duck, *Clangula hyemalis*. The male (inset: nonbreeding) has in common with the pintail a long tail visible in flight, but is set apart by a largely white back, a brown breast, and a stubby bill.

Breeding | Adult male

GREEN-WINGED TEAL

Anas crecca L 14½" (37 cm)

FIELD MARKS
Male's chestnut head has green
ear patch faintly outlined in white

Female has mottled, dusky brown
upperparts; white belly and
undertail coverts

In flight, shows green speculum
bordered above in buff

Behavior
Like other dabbling ducks, feeds at the water's surface
or upended, tail in the air and head submerged, to
reach aquatic plants, seeds, and snails. The Green-
winged has a specialized bill for filtering food from the
mud. An agile and fast-moving flier, travels in small
flocks that synchronize their twists and turns in midair.
The Green-winged female emits a high, shrill *skee*.

Habitat
Found on coastal estuaries and tidal marshes, and on
shallow lakes and inland ponds, especially those with
standing or floating vegetation. Nests are hidden
among grasses and weeds, within 200 feet of water.

Local Sites
Green-winged Teals are widespread in wetland habitats
throughout much of Washington and Oregon.

FIELD NOTES The Cinnamon
Teal, *Anas cyanoptera*, is strictly
a spring and summer visitor to
marshes, ponds, and lakes of
the area. The male (inset: breed-
ing) is easily separated from the Green-winged, but the females
can be more difficult to tell apart. In flight, though, both sexes of
Cinnamon Teal show a patch of pale blue on the upper wing.

Breeding | Adult male

RING-NECKED DUCK

Aythya collaris L 17" (43 cm)

FIELD MARK

Male has black head, breast, back, and tail; pale gray sides

Female is brown with pale face patch, eye ring, and eye stripe

Peaked crown; blue-gray bill with white ring and black tip

Behavior

An expert diver, the Ring-necked can feed as deep as 40 feet below the surface, but tends to remain in shallower waters. Small flocks can be seen diving in shallow water for plants, roots, and seeds. Unlike most other diving ducks, the Ring-necked springs into flight directly from water, and flies in loose flocks with rapid wing beats. Though often silent, the Ring-necked hen sometimes gives a harsh, grating *deeer*.

Habitat

Inhabits freshwater marshes, woodland ponds, and small lakes. Found in coastal marshes in winter. Often nests atop a floating raft of aquatic vegetation.

Local Sites

Ring-neckeds tend toward the coast in winter and disperse inland to breed. Nisqually National Wildlife Refuge in Washington is one place to find them all year.

FIELD NOTES The Lesser Scaup, *Aythya affinis* (inset: breeding male, left; female, right) can be distinguished from the Ring-necked by its bluish gray bill. It is found in wetlands across Washington and Oregon, primarily in winter. The Lesser's larger cousin, the Greater Scaup, *Aythya marila*, stays on the coast and larger bodies of water and visits only in winter. It has a more rounded crown.

Breeding | Adult female, left; adult male, right

HARLEQUIN DUCK

Histrionicus histrionicus L 16½" (42 cm)

FIELD MARKS
Breeding male has dark body
marked with white lines and
patches and chestnut flanks

Female is dark brown with three
white spots on each side of head

Nonbreeding male and juvenile
resemble female

Behavior
This small sea duck dives for its food, using both feet
and wings for propulsion underwater. Feeds primarily
on aquatic insects, crustaceans, and mollusks. In winter, known to pry barnacles from the rocky cliffs of the
coast. Often flies low over water. Though usually silent,
male gives a high-pitched nasal squeaking during
courtship, and both sexes may sometimes emit low-
pitched croaks.

Habitat
In winter, remains near rocky cliffsides along the coast.
Migrates inland to fast-moving mountain streams for
breeding. Nests are built close to water, hidden among
rocks and brush, or in hollowed-out logs.

Local Sites
Harlequin Ducks are most easily found in winter near
coastal rocks or jetties such as those at Yaquina Bay in
Oregon, or in Puget Sound near spots such as Ediz
Hook in Port Angeles, Washington.

FIELD NOTES Though ornately patterned at close range, the breeding
Harlequin drake can appear quite dark from a distance, especially
when at rest. Scan large rocks that jut out of the more turbulent mountain streams of the Cascade range for this small duck's bright white
patch in front of his eye.

Year-round | Adult male

SURF SCOTER

Melanitta perspicillata L 20" (51 cm)

FIELD MARKS
Male black overall, bold white forehead and nape patch; black, white, red, and yellow bill

Female brown with two white patches on each side of head

Distinctly sloping forehead

Behavior
A true sea duck found wintering along the coast of the entire region. Forages by diving, mainly for mollusks such as clams and mussels. Large flocks assemble at favorable feeding locations, particularly at low tide when food is more accessible. Bold black-and-white head pattern earned this elegant duck the inappropriate sobriquet of "skunkhead." Though usually silent, sometimes emits low-pitched, gurgling notes.

Habitat
Large flocks winter along the coast in shallow marine water or in coastal bays and sounds. Breeds on the subarctic tundra.

Local Sites
This duck is abundant and widespread in salt water along Washington and Oregon's coastline from fall through spring.

FIELD NOTES Two other scoters share the Surf Scoter's wintering grounds, the White-winged Scoter, *Melanitta fusca* (inset; male, left; female, right), identifiable by its black plumage, white wing patch, and the male's spot of white by his eye; and the Black Scoter, *Melanitta nigra*. The male Black Scoter is all-black with a bright yellow-orange knob on its otherwise black bill.

Breeding | Adult male

BUFFLEHEAD

Bucephala albeola L 13½" (34 cm)

FIELD MARKS

Small duck with large puffy head, steep forehead, and short bill

Male has large white head patch and a glossy black back

Female is gray-brown overall with small, elongated white patches on either side of her head

Behavior

Often seen in small flocks, some birds keeping a lookout on water's surface while others dive for aquatic insects, snails, and small fish. Like all divers, feet are set well back on its body to swiftly propel it through water. Takes off directly out of water, unlike many other diving ducks. Buffleheads are believed to stay with the same mate for years and to faithfully return to the same nesting site each season. Male's call is a squeaky whistle, female emits a harsh quack.

Habitat

Found on sheltered bays, rivers, and lakes. Nests only in isolated pockets of Washington and Oregon, almost exclusively in cavities created by the Northern Flicker.

Local Sites

Widespread throughout Washington and Oregon in winter, the coastal bays of both states are particularly good spots to scan for flocks of these small ducks.

FIELD NOTES The large white head patch of the adult male Hooded Merganser, *Lophodytes cucullatus* (inset), can be mistaken for that of the Bufflehead from a distance. Look for this merganser's buffy flanks and its thin serrated bill, specialized for capturing fish underwater.

Breeding | Adult male and female

COMMON MERGANSER

Mergus merganser L 25" (64 cm)

FIELD MARKS

Breeding male has blackish green head and black back

Female and nonbreeding male have chestnut head and gray back

Long, slim neck

Thin, hooked red bill

Behavior

Swiftly gives chase to small fish underwater. A long, thin, serrated bill helps it to catch fish, mollusks, crustaceans, and aquatic insects. Flies low with rapid wing beats, following the course of rivers and streams. Pairs form in late winter, before which this bird is most commonly found in single-gender flocks of 10 to 20 birds. Harsh croaks can be heard from the drake; a loud, harsh *carr-carr* from the hen.

Habitat

Prefers the still, open water of large lakes, but may also be found in rivers of wooded areas, especially in winter. Nests in woodlands in tree cavities, and rock crevices near lakes and rivers.

Local Sites

Common Mergansers can be found on large bodies of water throughout most of Washington and Oregon year-round. Anywhere along Nisqually River in Washington is fairly reliable.

FIELD NOTES The female Red-breasted Merganser, *Mergus serrator* (inset), is similar to the female Common Merganser, but note the Red-breasted's paler head and neck without a distinctly outlined white throat.

Year-round | Adult male

RING-NECKED PHEASANT

Phasianus colchicus Male L 33" (84 cm) Female L 21" (53 cm)

FIELD MARKS

Male iridescent bronze, mottled with black, brown, and gray

Female buffy overall with dark spotting and barring

Male has fleshy red eye patches

Long tail; short, rounded wings

Behavior

This introduced Asian species feeds primarily on seeds and grain, but will also eat weeds, buds, berries, and insects. Like other game birds, the Ring-necked has a crop in which it stores food, reducing the amount of time required for it to forage in the open. Generally tends to run, rather than fly, but if flushed, this bird rises almost vertically with a loud whirring of its wings. Male's territorial call is a loud, penetrating *kok-kak*.

Habitat

Prefers open country, farmlands, brushy areas, or woodland edges. Nests on the ground in a shallow depression made by the female.

Local Sites

A year-round resident within its range, the Ring-necked Pheasant is most numerous in agricultural areas of eastern Washington and Oregon.

FIELD NOTES The Ruffed Grouse, *Bonasa umbellus* (inset), is another member of the family Phasianidae. It occurs in wooded stretches of Washington and Oregon. It is light brown, or less commonly gray, overall with a small crest and a multibanded tail. In spring, listen for the male's "drumming" display, produced by rapidly beating wings.

Year-round | Adult male

CALIFORNIA QUAIL

Callipepla californica L 10" (25 cm)

FIELD MARKS
Mostly gray above, brown
sides with white streaks, scaled
underparts

Prominent teardrop-shaped plume,
larger on male

Black throat and chin bordered in
white on male

Behavior
Primarily a ground feeder, forages mainly on seeds,
flowers, buds, and other plant material. Will sometimes
consume spiders, snails, beetles, and other insects.
Often visits platform feeders or lawns with scattered
seeds, usually around sunrise or sunset. Prefers running
to flying, but will flush to escape predators. Pairs off to
breed, but may be seen in fall in coveys numbering up
to 100 birds. Calls include a loud, emphatic *chi-ca-go*
and varied grunts and cackles.

Habitat
Widespread and common in open woodlands, brushy
foothills, and sagebrush scrublands, usually near a
permanent water source. This species has also adapted
well to man-made habitats and can be found in
suburbs. Female builds simple nest on the ground.

Local Sites
Malheur National Wildlife Refuge in Oregon and
Dungeness National Wildlife Refuge in Washington are
two good spots to find this dapper New World Quail.

FIELD NOTES These quails are known to return to the same spots
to feed, including lawns and gardens, as long as the source of
food remains available. Among a foraging covey, look for one
bird standing guard from a perch while the others feed. In the
case of a new brood, the guard bird is invariably the adult male.

Nonbreeding | Adult

COMMON LOON

Gavia immer L 32" (81 cm)

FIELD MARKS

Dark gray above, pale below

Blue-gray bill

Dark nape has white indentation on each side

Back is checkered black-and-white in breeding plumage

Behavior

A diving bird; eats fish up to 10 inches long, which it grasps with its pointed beak. Forages by diving and swimming underwater, propelled by large, paddle-shaped feet. Can stay submerged for up to three minutes at depths down to 250 feet. It is nearly impossible for the Common Loon to walk on land. Generally remains silent on wintering grounds. Listen for its loud yodeling call on breeding grounds.

Habitat

Winters in coastal waters, or slightly inland on large bodies of water. Nests near large wooded lakes.

Local Sites

The Common Loon breeds on some large bodies of water in Washington. In winter, the best place to look for it, and the Red-throated Loon, is on coastal bays or along Puget Sound.

FIELD NOTES The eponymous brick red throat patch of the Red-throated Loon, *Gavia stellata* (inset: nonbreeding), is visible only during breeding season. In winter, in waters off Washington and Oregon's coast, the Red-throated can be identified by the sharply defined white on its face, which extends farther back than that of the Common Loon, and by its habit of holding its thinner bill angled slightly upward.

Breeding | Adult

PIED-BILLED GREBE

Podilymbus podiceps L 13½" (34 cm)

FIELD MARKS
Small and short-necked

Breeding adult brownish gray
overall; black ring around stout,
whitish bill; black chin and throat

Winter birds lose bill ring; chin
becomes white; plumage is
browner overall

Behavior
The most widespread of North American grebes, the
Pied-billed remains for the most part on water, seldom
on land or in flight. When alarmed, it slowly sinks,
holding only its head above the water's surface. Its bill
allows it to feed on hard-shelled crustaceans, breaking
apart the shells with ease. Pursues fish underwater and,
once prey is grasped in its bill, will eat it whole while
still submerged. Lobed toes make grebes strong
swimmers. Call is a loud *cuk-cuk-cuk* or *cow-cow-cow*.

Habitat
This widespread bird prefers nesting near freshwater
marshes and ponds. Also found in more open waters of
large bays and rivers, where it dives to feed on aquatic
insects, small fish, frogs, and vegetable matter. Winters
on both fresh and salt water.

Local Sites
The Pied-billed can be found year-round at a number
of wetland sites, such as Eastmoreland Park in Portland,
Siltcoos Lake on Oregon's coast, and Green Lake and
Juanita Bay Park not far from Seattle.

FIELD NOTES Like most grebes, the Pied-billed eats its own
feathers and feeds them to its young, perhaps to protect their
stomach linings from fish bones or animal shells.

Year-round | Adult

WESTERN GREBE

Aechmophorus occidentalis L 25" (64 cm)

FIELD MARKS

Striking black-and-white plumage

Large; long, thin neck

Black cap extends below eye

Paler plumage around eye in winter

Long, pointed, yellow-green bill

Behavior

Feeds almost exclusively on fish, which it pursues and often consumes underwater. Like herons, this grebe can snap its long neck instantaneously forward to strike or spear prey with its long, pointed bill. In courtship, a pair will rise up and rush side by side for great distances across the surface of the water. Call is a loud two-note *crick-kreek*.

Habitat

Breeds mainly inland on freshwater lakes and wetlands, where emergent vegetation borders open water. A pair cooperates in building a floating nest, anchored to the vegetation. In winter, most move to coastal salt and brackish marshes, estuaries, bays, and sheltered coves.

Local Sites

Reliable spots to view the Western Grebe's elaborate courtship ritual are Klamath Lake in Oregon and Potholes Reservoir in Washington.

FIELD NOTES The Horned Grebe, *Podiceps auritus* (inset: nonbreeding), is an uncommon breeder in Washington and Orgeon, but can be found in winter in saltwater estuaries along the coast. It is considerably smaller than the Western, with a shorter, blunter bill and a less starkly black-and-white pattern overall.

Breeding | Adult

BROWN PELICAN

Pelecanus occidentalis L 48" (122 cm)

FIELD MARKS

Exceptionally long bill with red throat pouch while breeding

Silvery gray above; blackish brown below; pale yellow crown and forehead

Breeding adult's hindneck is chestnut; winter adult's is white

Behavior

Dives from the air into water to capture prey. On impact, its throat pouch balloons open, scooping up small fish. Tilts its bill downward to drain water, tosses its head back to swallow. Sometimes gathers in groups over transitory schools of fish. Flocks travel low to the water in long, staggered lines, alternately flapping and gliding in unison. This species is currently making a significant recovery following a severe decline in its population due to pesticide poisoning. Generally silent.

Habitat

Largely coastal, the Brown Pelican summers along the shoreline in sheltered bays and near beaches.

Local Sites

The mouth of the Columbia River and Tillamook Bay are good places in Oregon to find the Brown Pelican in late summer. In Washington, try Grays Harbor or Willapa Bay.

FIELD NOTES The American White Pelican, *Pelecanus erythrorhynchos* (inset: breeding), shares the exceptionally long bill of the Brown Pelican, but is largely white with black flight feathers. It breeds locally at inland lakes and rivers in eastern Washington and Oregon.

Breeding | Adult

DOUBLE-CRESTED CORMORANT

Phalacrocorax auritus L 32" (81 cm) WS 52" (132 cm)

FIELD MARKS

Black overall; facial skin yellow-orange; pale bill hooked at tip

Distinctive kinked neck in flight

Breeding adult has tufts of white feathers behind eyes

Immature has pale neck and breast

Behavior

After locating prey, the Double-crested Cormorant can dive to considerable depths, propelling itself with fully webbed feet. Uses its hooked bill to grasp fish. Feeds on a variety of aquatic life. When it leaves the water, it perches on a branch, dock, or piling and half-spreads its wings to dry. Soars briefly at times, its neck in an S-shape. May swim submerged to the neck, bill pointed slightly skyward. Sometimes emits a deep grunt.

Habitat

Found along coasts, at inland lakes, and near rivers; it adapts to fresh or saltwater environments. Nests near water either in trees or on rocks.

Local Sites

All three of the region's regular cormorants, the Double-crested, the Pelagic, and the Brandt's, are year-round residents along Washington and Oregon's coastline.

FIELD NOTES The Pelagic Cormorant, *Phalacrocorax pelagicus* (inset: breeding), shares the Double-crested's year-round range along Washington and Oregon's coastline. Between April and May, the Pelagic can be distinguished by its red facial skin, white flank patches, and breeding tufts; for the rest of the year, look for its thinner, darker bill and the greenish sheen on its body.

Breeding | Adult

GREAT BLUE HERON

Ardea herodias L 46" (117 cm) WS 72" (183 cm)

FIELD MARKS

Gray-blue overall; white foreneck
with black streaks; yellowish bill

Black stripe extends above eye

Breeding adult has plumes on its
head, neck, and back

Juvenile has dark crown; no plumes

Behavior

Often seen standing or wading along calm shorelines
or in rivers, foraging for food. It waits for prey to come
into its range, then spears it with a quick thrust of its
sharp bill. Flies with its head folded back onto its
shoulders in an S-curve, typical of other herons as well.
When threatened, draws its neck back with plumes
erect and points its bill at antagonist. Sometimes emits
a deep, guttural squawk as it takes flight.

Habitat

May be seen hunting for aquatic creatures in marshes
and swamps, or for small mammals inland, in fields
and forest edges. Pairs build stick nests high in trees in
loose association with other Great Blue pairs.

Local Sites

The Great Blue can be found in a variety of wetland
and agricultural areas for most of the year throughout
much of Washington and Oregon.

FIELD NOTES The name "crane" is often
mistakenly applied to the Great Blue Heron,
but cranes belong to an altogether different
family. The Sandhill Crane, *Grus canadensis* (inset),
can be seen in migration across the region; note its
protruding neck, which is held straight in flight as
opposed to the Great Blue's, which is drawn in.

Breeding | Adult

GREAT EGRET

Ardea alba L 39" (99 cm) WS 51" (130 cm)

FIELD MARKS

Large white heron with heavy
yellow bill, black legs and feet

Breeding adult has long plumes
trailing from its back, extending
beyond the tail

Blue-green lores while breeding

Behavior

Stalks its prey slowly and methodically, foraging in
shallow water with sharply pointed bill to spear small
fish, aquatic insects, frogs, and crayfish. Also known to
hunt snakes, birds, and small mammals. Occasionally
forages in groups or steals food from smaller birds.
Listen for the Great Egret's guttural croaking or its
repeated *cuk-cuk.*

Habitat

Inhabits both freshwater and saltwater wetlands. The
Great Egret makes its nest in trees or shrubs 10 to 40
feet above the ground. Colonies may have as many
as a hundred birds.

Local Sites

Malheur National Wildlife Refuge in Oregon and Potholes Reservoir in Washington are good sites to find
these birds breeding. In winter, try Fern Ridge Reservoir in Eugene, Oregon, or Baskett Slough National
Wildlife Refuge west of Salem, Oregon.

FIELD NOTES Early in the breeding season, the Great Egret grows
long, ostentatious feathers called aigrettes from its scapulars.
In the late 1800s, aigrettes were so sought after by the millinery
industry that Great Egrets were hunted nearly to extinction. The
grassroots campaign to end the slaughter later developed into
the National Audubon Society. Today, loss of wetlands continues
to limit the population of Great Egrets and other herons.

Year-round | Adult

GREEN HERON

Butorides virescens L 18" (46 cm) WS 26" (66 cm)

FIELD MARKS
Small, chunky heron with blue-green back and crown, sometimes raised to form shaggy crest

Back and sides of neck deep chestnut, throat white

Short yellow to orange legs

Behavior
Usually a solitary hunter, a Green Heron that lands near one of its kind is likely to be attacked. Look for the bird standing motionless in or near water, waiting for a fish to come close enough for a swift attack. The Green Heron spends most of its day in the shade, sometimes perched in trees or shrubs. When alarmed, it may make a show by flicking its tail, raising its crest, and elongating its neck, revealing streaked throat plumage. Its common cry of *kyowk* may be heard in flight.

Habitat
Found in a variety of wetland habitats but prefers streams, ponds, and marshes with woodland cover. Both sexes build nest in tree or shrub, generally not far from the ground.

Local Sites
Between April and September, look for this skulking bird along the Willamette River in Oregon and at Marymoor Park or Nisqually National Wildlife Refuge, both along Puget Sound in Washington.

FIELD NOTES An innovative hunter, the Green Heron will sometimes, though rarely, stand at the edge of shallow water and toss twigs, insects, even earthworms into the water as lures to attract unsuspecting minnows into its striking range. This is one of the few instances of tool use in the bird world.

Year-round | Adult

TURKEY VULTURE

Cathartes aura L 27" (67 cm) WS 69" (175 cm)

FIELD MARKS

In flight, two-toned underwings contrast and long tail extends beyond feet

Brownish black feathers on body; silver-gray flight feathers

Unfeathered red head; ivory bill

Behavior

An adept flier, the Turkey Vulture soars high above the ground in search of carrion and refuse. Rocks from side to side in flight, seldom flapping its wings, which are held upward in a shallow V, allowing it to gain lift from conditions that would deter many other raptors. Known to spread its wings wide while roosting. Well developed sense of smell allows the Turkey Vulture to locate carrion concealed in forest settings. Feeds heavily when food is available but can go days without if necessary. Generally silent, but will emit soft hisses and grunts while feeding.

Habitat

Hunts in open country, woodlands, farms, and also in urban dumps and landfills. Often seen over highways, searching for roadkill. Nests solitarily in abandoned buildings or hollow logs and trees.

Local Sites

Turkey Vultures can be seen throughout most of Washington and Oregon during the summer. Wooded areas in the foothills of the Cascades host a good number.

FIELD NOTES The Turkey Vulture's naked head is an adaptation to keep it from soiling feathers while feeding and therefore reduces the risk of picking up disease from carcasses.

Year-round | Adult

OSPREY

Pandion haliaetus L 22-25" (56-64 cm) WS 58-72" (147-183 cm)

FIELD MARKS

Dark brown above, white below; female has darker neck streaks

White head, dark eye stripe

Slightly arched in flight, wings appear bent back or "crooked"

Pale plumage fringing in juvenile

Behavior

Hunts by soaring, hovering, then diving down and plunging feet-first into water, snatching its prey with long, lethal talons. Feeds exclusively on fish. The Osprey is the only North American raptor with so specialized a diet, making it susceptible to accumulating contaminants, such as pesticides. Call is a series of clear, resonant, whistled *kyew*s. During breeding season, a male Osprey may call to draw a female's attention to a prized fish hooked in his talons.

Habitat

Forages in a variety of aquatic habitats, including lakes, rivers, and reservoirs. Nests near bodies of fresh or salt water. Bulky nests are built atop dead trees or on specialized man-made platforms. Highly migratory, this bird can be found on all continents except Antarctica.

Local Sites

Fern Ridge Reservoir near Eugene and Crane Prairie Reservoir near Bend are two spots in Oregon that host nesting pairs. The waterfront at Everett, Washington, also hosts a number of pairs in summer.

FIELD NOTES Female Ospreys tend to be larger than males, as in most species of eagles and hawks. This is an advantage while nesting as females do the majority of brooding and are able to take larger prey than the males.

Year-round | Adult, left; Third-year, right

BALD EAGLE

Haliaeetus leucocephalus L 31-37" (79-94 cm) WS 70-90" (178-229 cm)

FIELD MARKS
Distinctive white head and tail

Large yellow beak, feet, and eyes

Brown body

Juveniles mostly dark, showing
blotchy white on underwing
and tail

Behavior
A rock-steady flier, the Bald Eagle rarely swerves or tips
on its flattened wings; in fact, it rarely even needs to
flap them. Feeds mainly on fish, but sometimes on
carrion or small land mammals as well. May also steal
fish from other birds of prey. Bald Eagles lock talons
and cartwheel together through the sky in an elaborate
dance during courtship. Call is a weak, flat, almost
inaudible *kak-kak-kak*.

Habitat
This member of the sea-eagle group generally lives and
feeds along seacoasts or along rivers and lakes. Known
to perch on sandbars of rivers rich in salmon. Nests
solitarily in tall trees or on cliffs.

Local Sites
In winter, look for this majestic soarer at the mouth of
the Columbia River or at McNary Dam near Pendleton,
Oregon. Large concentrations can be found along the
Skagit and Nisqually Rivers in Washington year-round.

FIELD NOTES Entire populations of Bald Eagles were decimated
in the 20th century by the widespread use of DDT, a pesticide
that causes the thinning of egg shells in birds that inadvertently
ingest it. After the banning of this chemical in the 1970s, protection and restoration programs have effectively brought about a
significant recovery for our national bird.

Juvenile

SHARP-SHINNED HAWK

Accipiter striatus L 10-14" (25-36 cm) WS 20-28" (51-71 cm)

FIELD MARKS

Adult blue-gray above, reddish brown
streaks on neck, breast, and belly

Squared-off tail with narrow white tip

Thin, bright yellow legs and feet

Juveniles are brown above, white
below with brown streaking

Behavior

Preys chiefly on small birds, often engaging in ambush
maneuvers or aggressive pursuit even through thick
foliage and undergrowth. Flight consists of several
quick wing beats and a glide, its quick turns assisted
by a long, rudderlike tail. This small hawk is highly
aggressive, even against humans, when defending its
territory. A *kek-kek-kek* call can be heard when the bird
is alarmed.

Habitat

Found in mixed woodlands, but can also be seen
in the open, especially during migration. Nests are
substantial stick structures located in tall trees.

Local Sites

The Sharp-shinned can be found in the mixed woodlands of residential areas throughout
Washington and Oregon.

FIELD NOTES Distinguishing the Sharp-shinned
from the Cooper's Hawk, *Accipiter cooperii*
(inset: juvenile, top; adult, bottom), is one of
birding's classic challenges. Both species
are largely brown as juveniles; blue-gray
above, rufous below as adults. The Cooper's is slightly larger, has a more rounded tail,
and shows a longer neck in flight.

Year-round | Adult light morph

RED-TAILED HAWK

Buteo jamaicensis L 22" (56 cm) WS 50" (127 cm)

FIELD MARKS

Reddish tail on adults; immature has brown, banded tail

Light, dark, and intermediate morphs occur

Dark bar on leading edge of underwing on most birds

Behavior

Watch the Red-tailed Hawk circling above, searching for rodents, sometimes kiting, or hanging motionless on the wind. Uses thermals to gain lift and limit its energy expenditure while soaring. Perches for long intervals on telephone poles and other man-made structures, often in urban areas. Listen for its distinctive call, a harsh, descending *keee-eeer*.

Habitat

Seen in a variety of habitats from woods to prairies to farmland. Common at habitat edges, where field meets forest or wetlands meet woodlands, favored for the variety of prey found there. Nests in large trees, on cliffs, or on man-made structures.

Local Sites

The Red-tailed Hawk is widespread year-round throughout Washington and Oregon.

FIELD NOTES Found in Washington and Oregon only in winter, the Rough-legged Hawk, *Buteo lagopus* (inset: female), is also known to glide through the air on rising columns of hot air called thermals. In flight, note the dark "wrist marks" on the underwing and a dark belly band. Look for it in Skagit Game Range in Washington.

Year-round | Adult male

AMERICAN KESTREL

Falco sparverius L 10½" (27 cm) WS 23" (58 cm)

FIELD MARKS
Russet back and tail; streaks or
dots on pale underparts

Two black stripes on white face

Male has blue-gray wing coverts

Female has russet wing coverts
and russet streaks on her breast

Behavior
Feeds on insects, reptiles, and mice and other small
mammals. Hovers over prey by coordinating its flight
speed with the wind speed, then plunges down for the
kill. Will also feed on small birds, especially in winter.
Regularly seen perched on fences and telephone lines,
bobbing its tail with frequency. Has clear, shrill call of
killy-killy-killy.

Habitat
North America's most widely distributed falcon. Found
in open country and in cities, often "mousing" along
highway medians or guarding small pastures. Nests in
tree holes, barns, or man-made boxes using little or no
nesting material.

Local Sites
The most common species of falcon in the region,
American Kestrels can be found in most areas of
Washington and Oregon throughout the year.

FIELD NOTES Though abundant in Washington and Oregon, the
kestrel is still threatened by factors such as competition for
nesting holes with the introduced European Starling and the
increased use of rodenticides, which decreases the amount of
prey available. The kestrel readily accepts specialized nesting
boxes though, which helps to keep its numbers stable.

Year-round | Adult

PEREGRINE FALCON

Falco peregrinus L 16-20" (41-51 cm) WS 36-44" (91-112 cm)

FIELD MARKS
Blue-black crown and nape

Black extends below eye, forming distinctive "helmet"

Adult shows tawny wash below

Juvenile is brownish above; underparts heavily streaked

Behavior
This incredibly fast raptor hunts by flying high on powerful wingbeats, then swooping in on prey in a spectacular dive that can clock in at 175 mph or more. Also flies low over water to surprise waterfowl prey. Feeds primarily on birds, the larger of which may be knocked out of the air and subsequently eaten on the ground. Though usually silent, gives out loud *kak-kak-kak* call if alarmed.

Habitat
Inhabits areas near cliffs; now also established in cities, nesting on bridges or tall buildings with very little nesting material. Though Peregrines tenaciously defend their territory during breeding season, they hunt over a much wider area and a variety of habitats in winter.

Local Sites
Resident Peregrines can be found at Cape Meares National Wildlife Refuge in Oregon and at Grays Harbor in Washington.

FIELD NOTES The Merlin, *Falco columbarius* (inset: male, left; female, right), is another fast, powerful, and aggressive falcon that visits Washington and Oregon primarily in the winter. It is smaller than the Peregrine and lacks the Peregrine's distinctive "helmeted" look.

Year-round | Adult

AMERICAN COOT

Fulica americana L 15½" (39 cm)

FIELD MARKS
Blackish head; slate gray body

Small, reddish brown forehead
shield; reddish eyes on adult

Whitish bill with dark band at tip

Greenish legs with lobed toes

Juvenile paler with darker bill

Behavior
The distinctive toes of the American Coot are flexible
and lobed, permitting it to swim well in open water
and even to dive in pursuit of aquatic vegetation and
invertebrates. It is also able to tip its tail up and stay
submerged to feed, like many ducks. Bobs its small
head back and forth when walking or swimming.
Forages in large flocks, especially during the winter.
Has a wide vocabulary of grunts, quacks, and chatter.

Habitat
Nests in freshwater marshes or in lakes and ponds on a
floating nest anchored to aquatic vegetation. Winters in
both fresh and salt water. The coot has also adapted to
human-altered habitats, including sewage lagoons for
foraging and suburban lawns for roosting.

Local Sites
Coots can be found in lowland aquatic habitats across
much of Washington and Oregon. They are one of the
most common breeding waterfowl in the region and
can be seen in the thousands during migration.

FIELD NOTES Its body too heavy for direct takeoff, the American
Coot's lobed toes help it to "run" on water. Accelerating with its
wings flapping rapidly, it is able to gain the speed it needs to
take flight.

Year-round | Adult

KILLDEER

Charadrius vociferus L 10½" (27 cm)

FIELD MARKS
Gray-brown above; white neck
and belly; two black breast bands

Black stripe on forehead and one
extending back from black bill

Red-orange rump visible in flight

Red orbital ring

Behavior
Often seen running, then stopping on a dime with an inquisitive look, then suddenly jabbing at the ground with its bill. Feeds mainly on insects that live in short vegetation. May gather in loose flocks, but more often seen by itself. The Killdeer's loud, piercing, eponymous call of *kill-dee* or its rising *dee-dee-dee* is often the signal for identifying these birds before sighting them. Listen also for a long, trilled *trrrrrrr* during courtship displays or when a nest is threatened by a predator.

Habitat
Although a type of plover—one of the shorebirds—the Killdeer prefers inland grassy regions, but also may be found along shorelines. Builds its nest on just about any spot of open ground, even in residential areas.

Local Sites
The Killdeer can be found in open areas throughout much of Washington and Oregon. Its numbers increase dramatically in the winter, once migrants arrive from points farther north.

FIELD NOTES If its nest is threatened by an intruder, the Killdeer is known to feign a broken wing, limping to one side, dragging its wing, and spreading its tail in an attempt to lure the threat away from its young. Once the predator is far enough away from the nest, the instantly "healed" Killdeer takes flight.

First Year

BLACK OYSTERCATCHER

Haematopus bachmani L 17½" (45 cm)

FIELD MARKS

Black to blackish brown plumage overall; darker on hood

Long, red-orange bill

Bright orange eye ring, yellow iris

Pinkish legs

Tip of bill is dusky for first year

Behavior

Feeds heavily on mussels, limpets, chitons, and occasionally on sea urchins or crabs—but not oysters, despite its name. When a bivalve parts its shells, the bird quickly inserts its bill, cuts the muscle, and feeds on the soft parts. Pairs are monogamous, known to use the same nest site for years. Call is a loud, piping whistle that can be heard even over the sound of waves.

Habitat

Found only in marine shoreline environments, favoring rocky over sandy areas. Breeds mainly on mixed sand and gravel shelves of rocky islands and headlands. Nest is made of shell fragments and small stones, collected mainly by male and formed into a shallow depression.

Local Sites

Black Oystercatchers can be found along the coast at sites like Yachats State Park in Oregon or Cape Flattery in Washington.

FIELD NOTES Though hard to confuse with the Black Oystercatcher, the Black Turnstone, *Arenaria melanocephala* (inset: nonbreeding), shares its rocky, coastal habitat. Look for it flipping aside shells and rocks to find insects hidden underneath.

Breeding | Adult

SPOTTED SANDPIPER

Actitis macularius L 7½" (19 cm)

FIELD MARKS
Olive-brown upperparts, barred
during breeding season

White underparts, heavily spotted
in breeding plumage

Short, straight orange bill tipped
in black

Short white wing stripe in flight

Behavior
Often seen singly, feeding on insects, crustaceans, and
other invertebrates by plucking them from the water's
surface or snatching them from the air. Walks with a
constant teetering motion. Generally stands with tail
up and head down. Flies with stiff, rapid, fluttering
wing beats, followed by glides. Calls include a shrill
peet-weet and a series of *weet* notes, given in flight.

Habitat
One of the most common and widespread sandpipers
in North America during breeding season, preferring
sheltered ponds, lakes, streams, or marshes. Nests on
grass near water. Winters in small numbers on rocky
shorelines of Oregon and southern Washington.

Local Sites
Look for Spotted Sandpipers during spring and
summer in wetland habitats throughout Washington
and Oregon, from the coast to the mountains and all
points in between.

FIELD NOTES The slightly larger female Spotted Sandpiper is
the first to establish territory and to defend it during breeding
season. She may also mate with several males in a single
season while the males tend to the eggs and young.

Nonbreeding | Adult

WHIMBREL

Numenius phaeopus L 17½" (45 cm)

FIELD MARKS
Gray-brown above mottled with
buff and white; whitish below

Long, dark, decurved bill with
pinkish base in winter

Boldly striped crown with dark eye
line and pale median strip

Behavior
Generally walks or runs as it probes the mud of tidal
areas with its long bill for insects, larvae, worms, mollusks, and crustaceans. Forages by itself, but may
be seen in flocks during migration. Call is a rapid series
of five to seven hollow whistles given in the same pitch.

Habitat
Generally stays close to the coast in winter and
migration. Stops over in Washington and Oregon at
coastal mudflats, sandy beaches, grassy or flooded
fields, and occasionally on the shores of inland lakes
and rivers. Breeds on open Arctic tundra.

Local Sites
Good places to find the Whimbrel during spring and
fall migration include Willapa Bay in Washington,
Yaquina Bay in Oregon, and at the mouth of the
Columbia River where the two states meet.

FIELD NOTES Though similar in appearance and foraging behavior, the range of the Long-billed Curlew, *Numenius
americanus* (inset), rarely overlaps in Washington or Oregon with that of the Whimbrel. The
Long-billed nests in grassy areas of eastern
Washington and Oregon and is characterized
by an even longer decurved bill.

Molting | Adult

SANDERLING

Calidris alba L 8" (20 cm)

FIELD MARKS

Pale gray above and white below
in winter; bill and legs black

Prominent white stripe and black
leading edge show on wing while
in flight

Juveniles black-and-white above

Behavior

Feeds on sandy beaches, chasing retreating waves in
order to snatch up newly exposed crustaceans and
mollusks, then darting back to avoid oncoming surf.
Migrating birds, seen in spring and early fall, have a
rusty wash on head and breast. Flies swiftly, aided by
ample wing length and sharp, pointed wings. Flocks
wheel and turn together in the air. Call is a sharp *kip*,
often emitted in a series.

Habitat

Winters on sandy beaches of the United States and
throughout most of the Southern Hemisphere. Some
birds migrate as many as 8,000 miles from remote
Arctic breeding grounds to southern South America.

Local Sites

The region's coastal sandy beaches are likely to host
Sanderlings in winter and migration. In late summer,
look as well for the juveniles.

FIELD NOTES Also to be found on
Washington and Oregon's coastal
beaches in winter, the Western
Sandpiper, *Calidris mauri* (inset: non-
breeding, left; juvenile, right), travels farther inland as well during
migration. It is slightly smaller than the Sanderling and not as
pale. Look as well for its longer bill, slightly drooped at the tip.

Nonbreeding | Adult

DUNLIN

Calidris alpina L 8½" (22 cm)

FIELD MARKS

Grayish brown upperparts; breast washed with gray-brown; white underparts

Long, stout, black bill, slightly decurved at tip

Black belly patch; rufous upperparts in breeding plumage

Behavior

Probes in shallows with a rapid up-down stitching movement of its bill, looking for insects, larvae, worms, snails, small fish, and crustaceans. A short neck makes this bird appear hunchbacked while foraging. A small but impressive flier, able to reach speeds of more than a hundred mph during migration. Large, rapidly moving flocks move through the air in synchronized flight. Distinctive call is a harsh, reedy *kree*.

Habitat

Migrates coastally as well as overland to winter in sandy, muddy, and rocky areas along North America's shorelines. Breeds in circumpolar Arctic tundra.

Local Sites

Estuaries such as those at Tillamook, Yaquina, and Coos Bay in Oregon and at Grays Harbor and Skagit Flats in Washington are good spots to scan for Dunlins.

FIELD NOTES Another drab-colored winter shorebird of Washington and Oregon is the Black-bellied Plover, *Pluvialis squatarola* (inset: nonbreeding). A good three inches larger than the Dunlin, it also has a relatively shorter bill. Both these birds molt in spring into distinctive breeding plumage: black-and-white for the Black-bellied; black, white, and rufous for the Dunlin.

Year-round | Adult

WILSON'S SNIPE

Gallinago delicata L 10¼" (26 cm)

FIELD MARKS
Stocky with very long bill; very
short tail; pointed wings

Head and back boldly striped
blackish brown and pale buff

Heavily barred flanks

Dark underwings, white belly

Behavior
Often not seen until flushed, when it gives harsh *ski-ape* call and rapidly flies off in a zigzag pattern. Feeds on insects, larvae, and earthworms by probing mud with its bill in a jerky fashion. Generally solitary, the snipe does not interact with other shorebirds. In swooping flight display, known as "winnowing," a quavering hoot-like sound is produced by air vibrating the two outermost tail feathers.

Habitat
Found in freshwater marshes and swamps and in any damp, muddy wetland where cover is afforded by vegetation. May frequent open areas as well. Nests on the ground in a scrape.

Local Sites
The Wilson's Snipe can be found breeding at wetland sites such as Malheur National Wildlife Refuge. In winter, it extends its range to the coast.

FIELD NOTES With a bill that can rival that of the Wilson's in length and straightness, the Long-billed Dowitcher, *Limnodromus scolopaceus* (inset: nonbreeding), is distinguished by its gray winter plumage, its V-shaped white patch extending up its back, and its tendency to remain in coastal areas.

Nonbreeding | Adult

RING-BILLED GULL

Larus delawarensis L 17½" (45 cm) WS 48" (122 cm)

FIELD MARKS

Yellow bill with black subterminal ring; pale eye with dark orbital ring

Pale gray upperparts; white underparts; yellowish legs; black primaries show white spots

Head streaked light brown in winter

Behavior

This opportunistic feeder will scavenge for garbage, grains, dead fish, fruit, and marine invertebrates. A vocal gull, it calls, croaks, and cries incessantly, especially during feeding. The call consists of a series of laughing croaks that begins with a short, gruff note and falls into a series of *kheeyaahhh* sounds. The Ring-billed takes three years to attain full adult plumage; immatures are marked by a varying amount of brown.

Habitat

Common in winter in coastal pastures, but also a regular visitor to most inland bodies of water, especially reservoirs in urban areas.

Local Sites

The Ring-billed Gull can be found circling over cities, parking lots, garbage dumps, and fast-food restaurants throughout its range.

FIELD NOTES The Mew Gull, *Larus canus* (inset: winter adult), is abundant in winter in Washington and Oregon, but remains mainly along the coast. It lacks the black ring of the Ring-billed, though immatures do have black tips on their bills. It is also marked in winter by a larger amount of brown on its nape and breast.

Breeding | Adult

WESTERN GULL

Larus occidentalis L 25" (64 cm) WS 58" (147 cm)

FIELD MARKS

Breeding adult has white head and underparts, dark gray mantle, and black primary tips

Head of nonbreeding adult is lightly streaked with brown

Large bill with red spot on lower mandible

Behavior

Catches fish by diving into water from air or by snagging them while wading. Often follows fishing boats to feed on discarded offal. Eats marine invertebrates, refuse, small mammals, and eggs of other birds. Drops shellfish onto ground from above in order to break the shell. Also known to steal fish from larger birds such as cormorants and pelicans. Call is a staccato *kaw-kaw-kaw*, lower-pitched than most other gulls.

Habitat

Remains strictly along the coast; most abundant at docks and towns along shoreline. Nests on rocks for the most part on offshore islands.

Local Sites

This bird is abundant along the coast year-round and in Puget Sound in the winter.

FIELD NOTES Like many other gulls, it takes four full years for a Western Gull to attain full adult plumage. It is largely brown with a dark bill as a juvenile and during its first winter (inset). By its second winter, it shows a mostly white head and belly and some gray in the mantle. By the third winter, it resembles an adult, but still has a dark bill tip as opposed to the red spot of the adult.

Nonbreeding | Adult

GLAUCOUS-WINGED GULL

Larus glaucescens L 26" (66 cm) WS 58" (147 cm)

FIELD MARKS

Breeding adult has white head
and underparts; pale gray mantle
and primaries

Nonbreeding adult marked with
light brown on head; upper breast
shows faint light brown barring

Red spot on lower mandible

Behavior

Like other gulls, dips for fish or catches them while
wading. Also eats marine invertebrates and small
mammals. Scavenges as well for leftovers from humans,
seals, and sea lions. The Glaucous-winged is one of the
major predators of eggs and young of colonies of other
birds within its range. Call a slow, slurred *kaw-kaw-kaw*.

Habitat

Found in a variety of coastal habitats, including bays,
estuaries, beaches, and mudflats. Also winters on
inland rivers and near garbage dumps. Nests on rocks
or sometimes on the roofs of waterfront buildings.

Local Sites

Any number of spots along Washington and Oregon's
coast will host good numbers of this gull in winter. In
summer, look for hybrids in Puget Sound.

FIELD NOTES The Glaucous-winged Gull hybridizes
with a number of other gull species, producing
considerable variations in plumage. Along the
Washington coast, Glaucous-winged x Western
hybrids may even outnumber pure birds. This hybrid
(inset: adult) shows a darker gray mantle and primary tips than
those of a pure Glaucous-winged Gull.

Breeding | Adult

CASPIAN TERN

Sterna caspia L 21" (53 cm) WS 50" (127 cm)

FIELD MARKS

Large, thick, red bill with dark tip

Pale gray above, white below

Breeding adult has black cap;
winter adult's crown is dusky

In flight, shows dark primary tips
and slightly forked tail

Behavior

Usually solitary, often hovers before plunge-diving for
small fish, its main source of food. The largest tern in
the world, the Caspian is quite predatory by nature,
frequently stealing catches from other gulls and terns,
and feeding on their eggs and chicks. Adult's calls
include a harsh *kowk* and *ca-arr*. Juvenile call is high,
thin whistled *whee-you.*

Habitat

Locally common and widespread on coastlines
throughout the world. Small colonies nest together
on beaches or on islands of inland rivers.

Local Sites

These birds can be found nesting at Grays Harbor in
Washington and on the tidal mudflats near Tacoma on
Puget Sound.

FIELD NOTES Named for a specimen first collected near the
Caspian Sea in Central Asia, this poweful flier occurs on most
of the world's landmasses, nesting across much of Eurasia
and North America and wintering in South America, India,
and Africa.

Nonbreeding | Adult

COMMON MURRE

Uria aalge L 17½" (45 cm)

FIELD MARKS
Black above, white below; head
can be a brownish black

Breeding adult has full black hood;
nonbreeding has white cheeks
partially crossed by a black line

Long, pointed, black bill

Behavior
Found out at sea, generally flying in long lines of 10 to
40 birds. Can dive hundreds of feet for fish and can stay
submerged for up to 60 seconds. Also eats marine
invertebrates such as squid and shrimp. Uses broad
wings to propel itself in search of prey, essentially
"flying" underwater. Though adults silent while on the
water, makes soft, nasal *murrr* sound in flight.

Habitat
Keeps to deep waters at all times except to breed. Colonies are located on rocky islands and cliff faces. Lays
pear-shaped egg on rocks with no nesting materials.

Local Sites
Look for Common Murres in winter from lookout
points on Puget Sound or year-round from Cape
Meares National Wildlife Refuge on the Oregon coast.

FIELD NOTES The Pigeon Guillemot, *Cep-
phus columba* (inset: breeding), is another of
the region's alcids, or "penguins of the north."
It can be found along Washington and Oregon's coast and in Puget Sound, primarily in
summer. While breeding, it is set apart from the Common Murre
by its mostly black plumage. In winter, it shows mostly white
underparts and retains its large, white wing patch.

Breeding | Adult

RHINOCEROS AUKLET

Cerorhinca monocerata L 15" (38 cm)

FIELD MARKS

Blackish brown above, paler on
sides, neck, and throat; white belly

Large, thick, yellow-orange bill;
short, thick neck

Breeding adult shows two white
facial stripes and a pale yellow
"horn" at the base of its bill

Behavior

Most often seen singly or in a small group. Stays far out
at sea and dives for small fish and crustaceans; able to
remain submerged for up to two minutes. Swims with
much of its body submerged and its head pulled in,
making it appear very thick-necked in the water. This
monogamous bird returns to the same nesting burrow
with the same mate every year in April. Though generally silent at sea, this bird gives throaty barks and
moans at breeding colony.

Habitat

Forages offshore above the continental shelf. Breeds
in colonies on islands, nests in soil burrows.

Local Sites

Look for Auklets in winter at Point Defiance in Tacoma
or on Puget Sound. Find breeding birds at Sea Lion
Caves, Oregon.

FIELD NOTES Though superficially resembling the penguins of the
Southern Hemisphere, the alcid family of the Northern Hemisphere is not closely related. Rather the similar body structure,
plumage coloration, and ability to use wings for underwater
propulsion are remarkable examples of convergent evolution—
similar adaptational responses to similar environments.

Breeding | Adult

TUFTED PUFFIN

Fratercula cirrhata L 15" (38 cm)

FIELD MARKS
Breeding male marked by white face, massive orange-red bill, and pale yellow head tufts

Nonbreeding adult has gray face, very short or absent tufts, and bill becomes shorter and drabber

Black overall; orange-red legs

Behavior
Forages at sea, chasing schools of fish and using its wings to propel itself underwater. Eats crustaceans, mollusks, and squid as well. Its body too heavy for direct takeoff, a Tufted Puffin must first run across water to gain the momentum needed to take flight. Generally silent at sea, this bird emits low, rumbling, throaty growls at breeding grounds.

Habitat
Forages and winters on offshore waters. Breeding colonies are located on rocks, islands, and cliffs along the coastline. Nests in small burrows dug into sand or soil, or sometimes in crevices between rocks.

Local Sites
Haystack Rock at Cannon Beach, Oregon, and offshore islands at Cape Flattery in Washington both host breeding colonies of Tufted Puffins in summer.

FIELD NOTES Auks, murres, and puffins are known to fly in straight lines, often with more than one species in a small flock. In general, the slowest in the flock will act as lead bird, and since puffins are slower in flight than murres, it is not a completely uncommon sight to find a single Tufted Puffin leading a short line of Common Murres.

Year-round | Adult

ROCK PIGEON

Columba livia L 12½" (32 cm)

FIELD MARKS

Variably plumaged, with head and neck usually darker than back

White cere at base of dark bill, pink legs

Iridescent feathers on neck reflect green, bronze, and purple

Behavior

Feeds during the day on grain, seeds, fruit, and refuse in cities, suburbs, parks, and fields; a frequent visitor to farms and backyard feeding stations as well. As it forages, the Rock Pigeon moves with a short-stepped, "pigeon-toed" gait while its head bobs back and forth. Courtship display consists of the male puffing out neck feathers, fanning his tail, and turning in circles while cooing; results in a pairing that could last for life. Characterized by soft *coo-cuk-cuk-cuk-cooo* call.

Habitat

Anywhere near human habitation. Nests and roosts primarily on high window ledges, on bridges, and in barns. Builds nest of stiff twigs, sticks, and leaves.

Local Sites

Introduced from Europe by settlers in the 1600s, the Rock Pigeon is now widespread and abundant throughout most developed regions of North America.

FIELD NOTES The Rock Pigeon's variable colors range from rust red to all white to mosaic (inset) due to centuries of domestication. Those resembling their wild ancestors have a dark head and neck, two black wing bars, a white rump, and a black terminal band on the tail.

Year-round | Adult

BAND-TAILED PIGEON

Patagioenas fasciata L 14½" (37 cm)

FIELD MARKS

Purplish head and breast

Dark-tipped yellow bill; yellow legs

Broad gray terminal tail band

Narrow white band on nape of adult, bordered below by a spot of greenish iridescence

Behavior

Often perches for long spans of time either singly or in a small group at the tops of trees with little or no foliage. Size of flock may increase in winter. Forages among branches for berries, grains, seeds, nuts, and insects; rarely descends to the ground. Call is a low, repetitive *whoo-whoo*, that sounds vaguely owl-like. During breeding season, male calls from an open perch to attract a mate.

Habitat

Found primarily in forests of tall coniferous trees located in montane or coastal areas. The Band-tailed is becoming increasingly common in suburban parks. Nests on platform of twigs in the fork of a tree.

Local Sites

Listen for the Band-tailed's owl-like calls, especially in spring and summer, in the forests of Washington and Oregon's coastal ranges.

FIELD NOTES One of only two native species of pigeons and doves in the northwestern United States, the Band-tailed was nearly hunted to extinction in the 20th century until restrictive measures were implemented in the 1980s. The species has recovered, but is still a cause of concern for conservationists.

Year-round | Adult male

MOURNING DOVE

Zenaida macroura L 12" (31 cm)

FIELD MARKS

Gray-brown; black spots on upper wings; white tips on outer tail feathers show in flight

Trim-bodied; long pointed tail

Black spot on lower cheek; pinkish wash on neck in male

Behavior

Generally a ground feeder, the Mourning Dove forages for grains, seeds, grasses, and insects. Like other *Columbidae*, it is able to slurp up water without tipping back its head. The Mourning Dove is aggressively territorial while nesting, but will gather into large roosting flocks after breeding season. Also known to produce multiple broods a season. Wings produce a fluttering whistle as the bird takes flight. Known for mournful call, *oowooo-woo-woo-woo*, given by males during breeding season.

Habitat

Widespread and abundant, the Mourning Dove is found in a variety of habitats, but prefers open areas, often choosing suburban sites for feeding and nesting.

Local Sites

Mourning Doves are common throughout most of Washington and Oregon, from wooded settings to farm fields to cities and towns. Oregon's Malheur National Wildlife Refuge is one particularly reliable spot.

FIELD NOTES The Mourning Dove, like other members of the family Columbidae, has the ability to produce "pigeon milk" in its crop lining. It regurgitates this substance to its young during their first few days. In appearance and nutritious content, it is remarkably similar to the milk of mammals.

Year-round | Adult

BARN OWL

Tyto alba L 16" (41 cm)

FIELD MARKS
White heart-shaped face

Dark eyes, pale bill

Rusty brown above, cinnamon-
barred wings

White to pale cinnamon spotted
underparts, darker on females

Behavior
A nocturnal forager of mice, small birds, bats, snakes, and insects. Hunts primarily by sound, often in pastures and marshes. Wing feathers with loosely knit edges and soft body plumage make its flight almost soundless, effective in surprising its prey. Roosts and nests in dark cavities in city and farm buildings, cliffs, and trees. Call is a harsh, raspy, hissing screech.

Habitat
Distributed throughout the world, this owl has adapted to the activities of man and is found in urban, suburban, rural, and other open regions throughout its range. Nests at all times of year in various sites, including tree hollows, barn rafters, burrows, or cliff holes.

Local Sites
Barn Owls inhabit lowland, non-forested regions throughout Washington and Oregon, but are most abundant in agricultural areas where old barns and bridges provide a suitable roosting environment.

FIELD NOTES Since it hunts primarily by sound, the Barn Owl is able to successfully locate its prey even in total darkness. Keeping one ear pointed upward and one downward, this owl's facial disc funnels in even faint sounds of scurrying mice.

Year-round | Adult

GREAT HORNED OWL

Bubo virginianus L 22" (56 cm)

FIELD MARKS
Mottled brownish gray above, densely barred below

Long ear tufts (or "horns")

Rust-colored facial disks

Yellow eyes; white chin and throat; buff-colored underwings

Behavior
Chiefly nocturnal. Feeds on a variety of animals including cats, skunks, porcupines, birds, snakes, grouse, and frogs; watches from high perch, then swoops down on prey. One of the earliest birds to nest, beginning in January or February, possibly to take advantage of winter-stressed prey. Call is a series of three to eight loud, deep hoots, the second and third often short and rapid.

Habitat
The most widespread owl in North America, the Great Horned Owl can be found in a wide variety of habitats including forests, cities, and farmlands. Reuses abandoned nests of other large birds.

Local Sites
A widespread species, look for the Great Horned in large trees throughout Washington and Oregon.

FIELD NOTES The Barred Owl, *Strix varia* (inset), inhabits a variety of woodlands throughout Washington and Oregon. During the 20th century, it has gradually expanded its range in the Northwest at the expense of the smaller Spotted Owl, with which it hybridizes. Its loud rhythmic call, *who-cooks-for-you*, *who-cooks-for-you-all*, is much more likely to be heard during the day than most owls' calls.

Year-round | Adult male

COMMON NIGHTHAWK

Chordeiles minor L 9½" (24 cm)

FIELD MARKS

Dark gray-brown mottled back; bold white bar across primaries

Long, pointed wings with pale spotting; tail slightly forked

Underparts whitish with bold dusky bars; bar on tail in males

Behavior
The Common Nighthawk's streamlined body allows agile aerial displays when feeding at dusk. Hunts in flight, snaring insects. Drops lower jaw to create opening wide enough to scoop up large moths. Skims over surface of lakes to drink. Roosts on the ground, scraping a shallow depression, or on branches, posts, or roofs. Call is a nasal *peent*. Male's wings make hollow booming sound during diving courtship display.

Habitat
Frequents woodlands and shrubby areas; also seen in urban and suburban settings. Nests on the ground or on gravel rooftops. Winters as far south as northern Argentina, making it one of the longest-distance migrants of any North American bird.

Local Sites
Between June and August, listen by night for the frog-like calls of this crepuscular species in open areas near water throughout Washington and Oregon.

FIELD NOTES The Common Nighthawk is common around mountain lakes. It will occasionally nest on flat, graveled roofs in towns and cities.

Year-round | Adult

VAUX'S SWIFT

Chaetura vauxi L 4¾" (12 cm)

FIELD MARKS
Stubby cigar-shaped body

Sooty gray-brown overall

Paler gray on throat and
upper breast

Spiky tips on rounded tail

Short, dark bill

Behavior
Almost exclusively seen in flight, flitting quickly with
rapid wing beats over cityscapes or over water in
wooded areas. Often seen in flocks circling over roofs
before dropping into chimneys to roost. Unable to
perch on its short, weak legs, this bird never descends
to the ground: it catches insects in flight, drinks and
bathes in flight, gathers nesting material in flight, even
breeds in flight. Call is a rapid, insect-like twittering.

Habitat
Nests in hollow trees of woodlands near water and has
recently adapted to nesting in chimneys and other hollow, man-made structures. Builds cup-shaped nest of
twigs, needles, and saliva. Winters in Central America.

Local Sites
Flocks can be seen circling over cities and towns of
Washington and Oregon in spring and summer.

FIELD NOTES Though not closely related, the Purple
Martin, *Progne subis* (inset: male), may also be found
circling swiftly in large flocks over wooded areas of
coastal Washington and Oregon. At close range, it is
clearly set apart by its iridescent blue plumage, but
from a distance look as well for its forked tail and its tendency to glide on fewer wing beats than the Vaux's Swift.

Year-round | Adult male

ANNA'S HUMMINGBIRD

Calypte anna L 4" (10 cm)

FIELD MARKS

Deep rose-red head, throat, and sides of neck in male

Female shows white throat speckled with red; green crown and nape

Green above, grayish below with varying amounts of green

Behavior

Hovers to gather nectar, catches flying insects, and is known to pluck spiders from their webs. May bathe by hovering against foliage covered with early morning dew. Considerably more vocal than most humming-birds, the Anna's common call note is a sharp *chick;* chase call a rapid, dry rattling; male's song a jumble of high squeaks and raspy notes, developed over time and incorporating various phrases and elements learned from neighbors.

Habitat

Found in coastal lowlands, suburban settings, and certain montane regions. Essentially nonmigratory, the range of this adaptable bird is expanding northward.

Local Sites

Specialized hummingbird feeders attract these birds in coastal suburban areas. The University of Washington Arboretum is also a good spot to find them.

FIELD NOTES At the beginning of the breeding season in early spring, look for the male Anna's courtship display. First he hovers in front of the female, then rises high, sometimes emitting a thin, squeaky song, then he executes an arching dive that ends in a loud *chirp* in front of the already partially built nest.

Year-round | Adult male

RUFOUS HUMMINGBIRD

Selasphorus rufus L 3¾" (10 cm)

FIELD MARKS

Male rufous above, rufous wash below; dark orange-red gorget

Female has green upperparts and white, speckled throat

Both show white breast patch extending down center of belly

Behavior

Makes one of the longest migrations relative to body size of any bird, needing frequent and expedient refueling. This highly aggressive hummer drives away competitors up to three times its size, including blackbirds, thrushes, even chipmunks. Courtship flight consists of male ascending with back to female, then diving and turning on its whistling wings with iridescent gorget showing. Calls include a *chip*, often given in a series, and a chase note of *zeee-chuppity-chup*.

Habitat

Found in summer wherever nectar can be found, especially in forested areas. Winters primarily in Mexico.

Local Sites

Both Rufous and Calliope Hummingbirds are drawn to backyard feeders. In general, the Rufous is found more often west of the Cascades, the Calliope farther east.

FIELD NOTES The female Calliope Hummingbird, *Stellula calliope* (inset: female, left; male, right) resembles the female Rufous in her green upperparts and pale buff underparts, but can be told apart by the lack of rufous in her tail and a higher-pitched *chip* call. The male differs from the Rufous in his streaked gorget and green upperparts.

Immature | Male

BELTED KINGFISHER

Ceryle alcyon L 13" (33 cm)

FIELD MARKS
Blue-gray head with large, shaggy crest

Blue-gray upperparts and breast band; white underparts and collar

Long, heavy, black bill

Chestnut sides and belly band in female

Behavior
Generally solitary and vocal, dives headfirst for fish from a waterside perch or after hovering above in order to line up on its target. Also feeds on insects, amphibians, and small reptiles. Both male and female carry out work in excavating nest tunnel, and share parenting duties. Mated pairs renew their relationship each breeding season with courtship rituals such as dramatic display flights, the male's feeding of the female, and vocalizations. Call is a loud, dry rattle; it is given when alarmed, to announce territory, or while in flight.

Habitat
Conspicuous along rivers, ponds, lakes, and coastal estuaries. Prefers partially wooded areas. Monogamous pairs nest in burrows they dig three or more feet into vertical earthen banks near watery habitats.

Local Sites
Belted Kingfishers can be found year-round throughout most of Washington and Oregon in riparian areas and protected wetland sites, such as Siletz Bay National Wildlife Refuge in Oregon.

FIELD NOTES The Belted Kingfisher female is one of the few birds in North America that is more colorful than her male counterpart, which lacks the female's chestnut band across the belly and chestnut sides and flanks.

Year-round | Adult

RED-BREASTED SAPSUCKER

Sphyrapicus ruber L 8½" (22 cm)

FIELD MARKS
Red head, nape, and breast

Black back spotted with white or yellow

Yellow to pale-yellow wash on belly

Large white wing patch in flight

Behavior
Drills even rows of holes in trees and strips bark to produce sap flow, then feeds on sap, insects it attracts, and berries. Often silent, it can emit a plaintive *mew* call in summer, but its biggest sound comes from the staccato pounding of its bill on wood, made possible by the well-adapted bone and muscle structure of its head, which can absorb a tremendous amount of shock.

Habitat
Found in damp, coniferous forests in coastal Pacific ranges. Northern race *ruber* nests in living deciduous trees at low elevations; southern race *daggetti* of southern Oregon nests in conifers, alders, and willows near water. Often uses old orchards in winter.

Local Sites
The Red-breasted can be found west of the Cascades in damp forests such as those found at Nisqually National Wildlife Refuge in Washington.

FIELD NOTES The Red-naped Sapsucker, *Sphyrapicus nuchalis* (inset: male, top; female, bottom), of eastern Washington and Oregon also drills rows of sap holes in trees, providing food for itself and a number of other woodlands animals. Its boldly patterned head sets it apart from the Red-breasted.

Year-round | Adult male

DOWNY WOODPECKER

Picoides pubescens L 6¾" (17 cm)

FIELD MARKS

Black cap, ear patch, moustachial stripe; black wings spotted white

White patch on back

White tuft in front of eyes; dusky whitish underparts

Red occipital patch on male

Behavior

The smallest woodpecker in North America forages mainly on insects, larvae, and eggs. Readily visits backyard feeders for sunflower seeds and suet. Will also consume poison ivy berries. Small size enables Downy to forage on smaller, thinner limbs. Both male and female stake territorial claims with their drumming. Call is a high-pitched but soft *pik*.

Habitat

Found in suburbs, parks, and orchards, as well as forests and woodlands. Nests in cavities of dead trees.

Local Sites

Widespread year-round throughout much of Washington and Oregon, but can be difficult to locate in dense woods. Downy Woodpeckers often frequent backyard feeding stations. Hairy Woodpeckers are much less common in suburban areas.

FIELD NOTES The larger and less common Hairy Woodpecker, *Picoides villosus* (inset: male), is similarly marked but has a bill as long as its head and a sharper, louder, lower-pitched call. It also tends to stay on tree trunks or larger limbs than the Downy. Note as well the all-white outer tail feathers of the Hairy Woodpecker; the Downy's outer tail feathers are often barred or spotted black.

Year-round | Adult male "Red-shafted"

NORTHERN FLICKER

Colaptes auratus L 12½" (32 cm)

FIELD MARKS
White rump; pinkish underwing

Brown, barred back; cream
underparts with black spotting;
black crescent bib

Gray crown, tan forehead;
red moustachial stripe on male

Behavior
Feeds mostly on the ground, foraging primarily
for ants. A cavity-nesting bird, the flicker drills into
wooden surfaces, including utility poles and houses.
Bows to its partner before engaging in court-ship
dance of exaggerated wing and tail movements. Call is
a single, loud *klee-yer* heard year-round or a loud series
of *wick-er, wick-er* during breeding season. The latter
call is sometimes repeated for up to 15 seconds.

Habitat
Prefers open woodlands and suburban areas with
sizeable living and dead trees. An insectivore, the
Northern Flicker is at least partially migratory,
traveling in the winter in pursuit of food.

Local Sites
The most common woodpecker in Washington and
Oregon, look for the Northern Flicker in lowland
and mountainous regions, wet and dry locales, rural
and urban areas.

FIELD NOTES The "Yellow-shafted" form of the Northern Flicker
is common in eastern North America. Its underwings and the
shafts of its flight feathers are yellow instead of pinkish red.

Year-round | Adult female

PILEATED WOODPECKER

Dryocopus pileatus L 16½" (42 cm)

FIELD MARKS

Almost entirely black on back and wings when perched

Black, white, and red striped head; red "moustache" on male

Red cap extends to bill on male

Juvenile browner overall

Behavior

Drills long, distinctively rectangular holes near bases of trees, then feeds on insects that sap attracts. Also digs into ground, stumps, and fallen logs, feeding on carpenter ants, beetles, acorns, nuts, seeds, and fruits. Male and female share in nesting and parenting duties. Flight call is a loud *wuk* note or series of notes. Territorial call is a longer series of laugh-like cackles. This bird is also known for its slow, but powerfully loud, territorial drumming, which can be heard from a mile or more away.

Habitat

Prefers dense, mature forests; also found in smaller woodlots and some parks. Nests in cavities excavated in dead or live trees, sometimes utility poles.

Local Sites

Pileated Woodpeckers are uncommon in hardwood and mixed forests throughout much of Washington and Oregon. Nisqually National Wildlife Refuge on Puget Sound is one reliable spot.

FIELD NOTES The ant-finding excavations of the Pileated Woodpecker are so extensive and deep that they may fell small trees. These holes also tend to attract other species of birds, such as small owls, wrens, and other woodpeckers, which use the large holes both for foraging and nesting.

Year-round | Adult

WESTERN WOOD-PEWEE

Contopus sordidulus L 6¼" (16 cm)

FIELD MARKS

Dark grayish above; paler below

Broad, flat, dark bill; yellow-orange at base of lower mandible

Two thin white wing bars; buffier on juvenile

Long, pointed wings

Behavior

Solitary and often hidden in trees. As it perches, it looks actively about, without flicking tail or wings. When prey is spotted, it darts out to catch a variety of flies, spiders, butterflies, wasps, ants, and dragonflies. Often returns to the same perch. Calls include a harsh, slightly descending *peeer,* and clear whistled *pee-yer.* Song is heard in spring and summer and has three-note *tswee-tee-teet* phrases mixed with *peeer* notes.

Habitat

Common in open woodlands and forest edges, especially in riparian areas. Female builds cup-shaped nest of grass, plant material, moss, and lichen on a horizontal branch of a tree. Winters in South America.

Local Sites

The Wood-Pewee can be found in summer in open wooded areas throughout the region.

FIELD NOTES The larger Olive-sided Flycatcher, *Contopus cooperi* (inset), is another summer visitor to wooded areas of the region. It shows a streaked vest and a white central breast. Note the Olive-sided's whiter throat and white tufts on the sides of its rump. Song sounds like a whistled *quick, three beers.*

Year-round | Adult

PACIFIC-SLOPE FLYCATCHER

Empidonax difficilis L 5½" (14 cm)

FIELD MARKS

Brownish green above, yellowish below; large olive-colored head

Broad bill with black upper mandible, orange lower mandible

Pale eye ring, broken above eye

Two pale wing bars

Behavior

Flycatchers are solitary and active birds, noted for perching in the upright position and often flicking wings and tail. With broad, hook-tipped bill, the Pacific-Slope Flycatcher snatches flying insects from its shaded perch and gleans insects from foliage. Leaves one perch to fly after food, then returns to a new perch. Female's call is a sharp *seet*, male's is a thin whistle. Song is an upslurred, repeated *psee-yeet*.

Habitat

Found in moist woodlands, coniferous forests, and shady forested canyons. Builds nest in a number of habitats from stream banks to porch eaves.

Local Sites

As its name suggests, this flycatcher is found in wooded areas on the Pacific side of the Cascades. It is also found east of the Cascades, where its range overlaps with the almost identical Cordilleran Flycatcher.

FIELD NOTES Six species of *Empidonax* flycatchers, or empids, regularly breed in Washington and Oregon. They are exceedingly difficult to tell apart—identifications rely on subtle field marks, vocalizations, and behavior. All of them, though, can be distinguished from Wood-Pewees (p. 139) by their habit of frequently flicking their wings and tails and constantly changing perches.

Year-round | Adult

SAY'S PHOEBE

Sayornis saya L 7½" (19 cm)

FIELD MARKS

Brownish gray above, darkest on head, wings, and tail

Tawny buff belly and undertail coverts

Adult has indistinct pale gray wing bars; juvenile's are cinnamon

Behavior

An active bird, the Say's rarely stays in one spot for long. Darts around in pursuit of flying insects and wags tail continually. Briefly perches on low-to-the-ground structures, such as branches, wires, and buildings. Song is often heard at dawn, consisting of two low-pitched, downslurred whistles, given alternately. Flight call is a quick *pit-tse-ar*. Typical call is a thin, whistled *pee-ee*.

Habitat

Unlike many flycatchers, the Say's inhabits dry, treeless areas such as sagebrush plains, dry foothills and canyons, and dry farmland. Uses mud pellets, plant material, and spider webs to attach nest to the vertical plane of a rock or building.

Local Sites

Look for the Say's in dry, open areas east of the Cascades. They arrive in the area in mid-February.

FIELD NOTES The Black Phoebe, *Sayornis nigricans* (inset: adult, top; juvenile, bottom), also hunts for flying insects from low perches, but is very much tied to habitats near water. It is easily distinguished from the Say's by its black body and white belly. Though its range is expanding, now it is found only in the southwest corner of Oregon.

Year-round | Adult

WESTERN KINGBIRD

Tyrannus verticalis L 8¾" (22 cm)

FIELD MARKS

Pale gray head, neck, and breast; lemon-yellow belly and underwing

Back tinged with olive

Black tail with white edges

Juvenile has buffy edges on wing coverts

Behavior

Feeds on flying insects, leaving perch to snag prey in midair. Food includes spiders, cicadas, grasshoppers, butterflies, and dragonflies. Perches horizontally, often on man-made structures such as fences, wires, and telephone lines. Courtship display involves animated aerial flights and singing. Common and gregarious, nesting pairs regularly share the same tree. Has a raspy call when defending territory—a sharp *whit*—and will chase away birds as large as hawks, crows, and ravens.

Habitat

Found in open habitats, including those near human habitation. Builds nest near the end of a horizontal tree branch. Winters primarily in central America.

Local Sites

Malheur National Wildlife Refuge is one spot among many in Washington and Oregon to find both Western and Eastern Kingbirds.

FIELD NOTES The Eastern Kingbird, *Tyrannus tyrannus* (inset), the "tyrant of tyrants," is so aggressive in defending its territory, it has even been known to pluck feathers from the backs of birds as large as vultures. It is largely black above and white below and is found in the eastern half of Washington and Oregon in summer.

Year-round | Adult

WARBLING VIREO

Vireo gilvus L 5½" (14 cm)

FIELD MARKS

Gray to olive-gray above, whitish to yellowish below

Gray eye stripe, paler above eye

Blue-gray bill, legs, and feet

No wing bars; crown does not contrast with back

Behavior

Seen singly or in a pair, this bird's drab gray plumage can be hard to spot while perched near the tops of large trees. Forages slowly and it is deliberately high up in trees for insects, caterpillars, larvae, and sometimes fruit. Call is a harsh, nasal *gwee*. Song is a long, choppy warble of up to 20 notes, often ending in a down-slurred *buzz*. Male is known to sing even while incubating eggs.

Habitat

Found for the most part in wooded riparian areas of deciduous forests. Cup-shaped nest hangs between the fork of a tree, generally toward the end of a branch.

Local Sites

This nondescript bird is a summer resident of deciduous forests throughout the area. Look for it along rivers and streams, as it almost always nests near water.

FIELD NOTES The Cassin's Vireo, *Vireo cassinii* (inset), like all vireos, has a short bill slightly hooked at the tip, which aids it in gleaning insects and in eating fruits. The Cassin's, a summer resident of Washington and Oregon's coniferous forests, can be distinguished from the Warbling Vireo by its white spectacles, its two whitish wing bars, and its lower-pitched, choppier song.

Year-round | Adult

GRAY JAY

Perisoreus canadensis L 11½" (29 cm)

FIELD MARKS
Dark gray upperparts; patch of
black on head

Whitish forehead, throat, and
cheeks; pale gray breast and belly

Short, black bill

Juvenile dark gray overall

Behavior
Feeds on a wide variety of prey, including small mammals, young birds and eggs, insects, seeds, nuts, and berries. Quite tame around humans, this bird will often steal food from campsites. Large salivary glands produce a mucus that allows this bird to store food by sticking it to trees. Male feeds female during courtship. Varied calls include a whistled *wheeoo,* a low *chuck,* and imitations of hawks.

Habitat
Found in high-elevation conifer forests of mountain ranges. Builds nest either on a branch near the trunk of a tree or in the crotch of a tree.

Local Sites
The Gray Jay almost exclusively inhabits the coastal ranges, the Cascades, and the Blue Mountains of Washington and Oregon. Crater Lake National Park is one good spot to look for it year-round.

FIELD NOTES Another inhabitant of high-elevation mountain ranges of Washington and Oregon is the Clark's Nutcracker, *Nucifraga columbiana* (inset). It is also commonly found attempting to steal food from campers. Look for its pale gray body, black wings, and its black-and-white tail.

Year-round | Adult

STELLER'S JAY

Cyanocitta stelleri L 11½" (29 cm)

FIELD MARKS

Black head, crest, back, and bill

Deep blue upperparts; paler blue underparts

Narrow black bars on wings and tail

Juvenile drabber overall

Behavior

Regularly seen in flocks and family groups. Bold and aggressive, often scavenges in campgrounds and picnic areas. Powerful bill efficiently handles a varied diet. Forages during warm months on insects, carrion, young birds, and eggs. Winter diet is mainly acorns and seeds. Highly social, jays will stand sentry, ready to mob predators, while others in the flock forage. Varied calls include a series of loud *shack* notes. Also known to imitate other birds, including hawks, thrashers, and loons.

Habitat

Found in woodland habitats, orchards, agricultural areas near woods, and residential areas. Nests in conifers, on a horizontal limb or in the crotch of a tree.

Local Sites

Steller's Jays can be found in all coniferous wooded regions of Washington and Oregon, and in a number of suburban areas as well.

FIELD NOTES There are at least two subspecies of Steller's Jay that are resident in Washington and Oregon. Look for the nominate *stelleri* race with blue streaks on its forehead and throat in the Cascades and coastal ranges. In the Blue Mountains, look for the interior *macrolopha* race with white streaks on its face.

Year-round | Adult

WESTERN SCRUB-JAY

Aphelocoma californica L 11" (28 cm)

FIELD MARKS

Dark blue upperparts; brownish gray back; grayish underparts

White eyebrow; dark eye patch

Whitish, streaked throat

Variable bluish band on chest

Juveniles have sooty gray hood

Behavior

Seen in pairs and small flocks, foraging on ground and in trees for insects, fruit, seeds, grain, eggs, young birds, and small reptiles and mammals. The Western Scrub-Jay's strong, stout bill allows for a wide-ranging diet. During breeding season, male hops around the female with his tail spread and dragging on the ground. This bold species is not shy around humans and will often emit its metallic call, a raspy *shreep,* in a short series.

Habitat

Increasing its range significantly over the past several decades, this bird can now be found in the scrublands for which it is named, as well as in deciduous woodlands and suburban areas. Both sexes build nest in tree or shrub using twigs, grass, and moss.

Local Sites

This bird is common and visible in the foothills and valleys between the Cascades and the coastal ranges.

FIELD NOTES Resourceful feeders, jays are known to store seeds and acorns in the ground for winter months when food is not as abundant. As many of these seeds and acorns are never recovered and then germinate, this habit is a major factor in the establishment and distribution of North America's forests.

Year-round | Adult

BLACK-BILLED MAGPIE

Pica hudsonia L 19" (48 cm)

FIELD MARKS

Black upperparts, breast, and undertail coverts

White sides and belly

White wing patches show in flight

Bluish iridescence on wings; greenish iridescence on long tail

Behavior

Forages on the ground in family flocks of up to a dozen birds, feeding on insects, larvae, and carrion, and sometimes on the eggs of other birds. In winter, flocks may number 50 or more birds. Hoards food for later consumption and is also known to collect shiny nonfood items such as aluminum foil, glass shards, and even silverware. Typical calls include a whining *mag* and a series of loud, harsh *chuck* notes.

Habitat

Inhabits open woodlands, thickets, rangelands, and agricultural areas. Nests and roosts in riparian areas with dense overgrowth.

Local Sites

Magpies are widespread, common, gregarious, and noisy in areas east of the Cascades.

FIELD NOTES A monogamous pair of Black-billed Magpies may stay together throughout the entire year and is known to reuse the same nest site year in and year out. On the limb of a bush or tree, the female builds a domed structure out of sticks and mud brought to her by the male. Within this structure is the more conventional cup-shaped nest of plant material, roots, and some hair. Other birds as well are known to utilize the magpie's dome for shelter and nesting.

Year-round | Adult

AMERICAN CROW

Corvus brachyrhynchos L 17½" (45 cm)

FIELD MARKS
Black, iridescent plumage overall

Broad wings; fan-shaped tail

Long, heavy, black bill

Brown eyes

Black legs and feet

Behavior
Often forages, roosts, and travels in flocks. Individuals take turns at sentry duty while others feed on insects, garbage, grain, mice, eggs, and young birds. Known to noisily mob large raptors such as eagles, hawks, and Great Horned Owls, in order to drive them from its territory. Because its bill is ineffective on tough hides, crows wait for another predator—or an automobile—to open a carcass before dining. Studies have shown the crow's ability to count, solve puzzles, and retain information. Readily identified by its familiar call, *caw-caw*.

Habitat
One of North America's most widely distributed and familiar birds, lives in a variety of habitats, including urban areas. Nests in shrubs, trees, or on poles.

Local Sites
Common throughout its range, crows can be seen almost anywhere, from farm fields to cities.

FIELD NOTES Where the American Crow's range drops off in coastal northwestern Washington, look for the almost identical Northwestern Crow, *Corvus caurinus*. Considered by some authorities to be a subspecies of the American Crow, the Northwestern is slightly smaller and has a lower, hoarser call. It inhabits beaches, islands, and coastal towns on Puget Sound.

Year-round | Adult

COMMON RAVEN

Corvus corax L 24" (61 cm)

FIELD MARKS

Glossy black overall with iridescent violet sheen

Long, heavy, black bill with long nasal bristles on upper mandible

Thick, shaggy throat feathers

Wedge-shaped tail

Behavior
The largest perching bird in North America, the raven forages on a great variety of food, from worms and insects to rodents and eggs to carrion and refuse. Small groups are known to hunt together in order to overcome prey that is too large for just one bird to take. Monogamous for life, these birds engage in acrobatic courtship flights of synchronized dives, chases, and tumbles. Calls are extremely variably pitched, from a deep croak to a high, ringing *tok*.

Habitat
One of the most widespread species in the Pacific Northwest, the raven can be found in a variety of habitats, but is more abundant at higher elevations. Builds nest high up in trees or on cliffs.

Local Sites
The raven is most common east of the Cascades in undeveloped areas at high elevations.

FIELD NOTES Though the raven is considerably larger than the American Crow, this can be difficult to discern from a distance. Look as well for the raven's wedge-shaped tail, as opposed to the more squared-off tail of the crow. The raven is also much more likely to soar on flattened wings than the crow, which flies with very steady wingbeats.

Year-round | Adult male

HORNED LARK

Eremophila alpestris L 6¾-7¾" (17-20 cm)

FIELD MARKS

White or yellowish forehead bordered by black band, which ends in hornlike tufts on adult males

Black cheek stripes, bill, and bib

Yellow or white throat and underparts; brown or rufous upperparts

Behavior

Forages on the ground, favoring agricultural fields with sparse vegetation. Feeds mainly on seeds, grain, and some insects. Male performs courtship flight display, ascending several hundred feet, circling and singing, then plummeting headfirst toward the ground, flaring his wings open for landing at the last second. With horns upraised, he then struts for the female. Song is a weak twittering; calls include a high *tsee-ee* or *tsee-titi*.

Habitat

Prefers open grasslands, dirt fields, sod farms, airports, gravel ridges, and shores. Uses its bill and feet with long hind claws to create shallow depressions for nesting.

Local Sites

Hart Mountain in Oregon and Mount Rainier in Washington are both good for viewing the Horned Lark's spectacular flight display.

FIELD NOTES Another bird of the open field and sandy beach is the American Pipit, *Anthus rubescens* (inset: nonbreeding, left; breeding, right). The pipit winters along the coast and breeds in the higher elevation mountain ranges of Washington and Oregon. Look for its grayish brown upperparts, its thin bill and long legs, and its tail-bobbing habit.

Year-round | Adult male

VIOLET-GREEN SWALLOW

Tachycineta thalassina L 5¼" (13 cm)

FIELD MARKS
Dark above with green sheen on head and back; violet sheen on nape, wings, and tail in good light

White below and on face, extending above eye

Pointed wings; notched tail

Behavior
Usually feeds in a flock, taking flying insects by darting close to the ground or low over water, but may also be seen hunting at greater heights. Perches in long rows high up in trees and on fences or wires. Sometimes nests in loose colonies of up to 20 pairs. Call is a rapid, twittering *chi-chit*; song is a repeated *tsip-tsip-tsip*, most often given in flight around dawn.

Habitat
Found in canyons, cliffs, and urban areas. Nests in holes in trees, crannies in buildings, rock crevices, and man-made nest boxes. Diligently lines its nest with white feathers.

Local Sites
Widespread throughout the area, these birds are early spring migrants and congregate in lowland riparian areas when they first arrive from farther south.

FIELD NOTES The Tree Swallow, *Tachycineta bicolor* (inset: male), is a close relative of the Violet-green and is often found in the same flock. It is bright blue-green above, extending below the eye, stark white below, and its rump does not show as much white as the Violet-green's. Its voice is clearer and sweeter.

Year-round | Adult

CLIFF SWALLOW

Petrochelidon pyrrhonata L 5½" (14 cm)

FIELD MARKS
Blue-black crown, whitish forehead, chestnut throat and cheeks

Blue-black back with faint white streaks; whitish underparts

Squarish tail and buffy rump show in flight

Behavior
Primarily takes flying insects, but sometimes forages in shrubs or on ground for berries and fruit. Breeds in colonies of up to 1,000 birds in gourd-shaped nests (opposite) made of mud pellets, which the birds roll up in their bills and plaster to the sides of cliffs and buildings or underneath bridges and overpasses. Once Cliff Swallows depart for South America, wintering species readily take up the nests as roosting sites. Call is a low, husky *churr;* alarm call within the colony is a low *veer;* chattering song consists of creaks, squeaks, and rattles.

Habitat
Found in open riparian areas near cliffs, bridges, or buildings, but does not take well to overly developed settings. Usually migrates along waterways.

Local Sites
Rivers east of the Cascades with nearby cliffs house the densest colonies in Washington and Oregon.

FIELD NOTES The Northern Rough-winged Swallow, *Stelgidopteryx serripennis* (inset) is another summer breeder from farther south. It is drabber than the Cliff, dull brown above and white below, and it nests in burrows dug fairly deep into suitable soil throughout Washington and Oregon.

Year-round | Adult male

BARN SWALLOW

Hirundo rustica L 6¾" (17 cm)

FIELD MARKS

Long, deeply forked, dark tail

Iridescent deep blue upperparts;
cinnamon to whitish underparts,
paler on female

Rusty brown forehead and throat;
dark blue-black breast band

Behavior

An exuberant flyer, the Barn Swallow is often seen in
small flocks skimming low over the surface of a field or
pond, taking insects in midair. Will follow tractors and
lawn mowers to feed on flushed insects, many of which
are harmful to crops. An indicator of coming storms,
as barometric pressure changes cause the bird to fly
lower to the ground. Call is a short, repeated *wit-wit*.
Song is a husky warble interrupted by rattling creaks.

Habitat

Frequents open farms and fields, especially near water.
Has adapted to humans to the extent that it now nests
almost exclusively in structures such as barns, bridges,
culverts, and garages. Widely distributed across the
world, this bird also breeds in Europe and Asia and it
winters in South America and southern Africa.

Local Sites

No barn, bridge, or culvert is complete without a
couple of nesting pairs of Barn Swallows in summer.

FIELD NOTES Though the Barn Swallow nests in small colonies,
competition between breeding pairs can be stiff. With its nest
only inches from a neighboring nest, the male Barn Swallow vig-
orously defends his small territory. Unmated males have even
been known to kill the nestlings of a mated pair in an attempt to
break up the couple and mate with the female.

Year-round | Adult

BLACK-CAPPED CHICKADEE

Poecile atricapillus L 5¼" (13 cm)

FIELD MARKS
Black cap and bib

White cheeks

Grayish upperparts

Whitish underparts with rich buffy flanks, more pronounced in fall

Flight feathers edged in white

Behavior

A common backyard bird, the Black-capped Chickadee is often the first to find a new bird feeder. Also forages on branches and under the bark of various trees. Diet consists mostly of seeds, but eats some insects as well, and will hide food in different locations for later consumption. Calls include a low, slow, *chick-a-dee-dee-dee*. Song is a variable, clear, whistled *fee-bee* or *fee-beeyee*, the first note higher in pitch. Female at nest emits snake-like hissing if threatened.

Habitat

Common in open woodlands, clearings, and suburbs. Builds its nest of moss and animal fur in cavities in rotting wood or seeks out a man-made nest box.

Local Sites

The Black-capped Chickadee can be found in wooded suburban areas in much of Washington and Oregon.

FIELD NOTES The similarly plumaged Mountain Chickadee, *Poecile gambeli* (inset), is not quite as domestic as its cousin, keeping primarily to less developed, higher altitude locales. It has a distinctive white eyebrow that can become obscured in summer. Look also for its grayer underparts and the grayer edging to its flight feathers.

Year-round | Adult

CHESTNUT-BACKED CHICKADEE

Poecile rufescens L 4¾" (12 cm)

FIELD MARKS

Black cap and chin; white cheeks

Chestnut back and rump

Grayish underparts, washed
with variable amount of chestnut
on flanks

White edging to flight feathers

Behavior

Forages high up in trees in small family groups during
summer and in larger mixed-species foraging flocks in
winter. Eats primarily insects and larvae, but also spiders, fruits, and seeds. Will descend to ground to scour
decaying logs for insects or to visit feeders. Call is a
hoarse, rapid *tseek-a-dee-dee*. Song is a series of *chip*s.
Female at nest emits snake-like hissing if threatened.

Habitat

Most often found in conifer forests, but may also use
mixed woodlands. Nest built in tree using plant material, fur, and feathers.

Local Sites

These birds are abundant in the mature conifer forests
of the Coast Range, the Cascades, and their foothills.

FIELD NOTES Like other chickadees, the Chestnut-backed is
known to join in mixed-species foraging flocks after the breeding
season. Consisting at times of kinglets, nuthatches, creepers,
warblers, vireos, and Downy Woodpeckers, these groups flit from
tree to tree as they comb through the trunks and vegetation of a
patch of woods. This practice helps to prevent the birds from foraging in areas that have recently been picked clean of food.

Year-round | Adult male

BUSHTIT

Psaltriparus minimus L 4½" (12 cm)

FIELD MARKS

Drab gray above, paler below
sometimes with a buffy wash

Brown cap

Males have dark eyes; females
pale irises and distinct pupils

Short black bill; long tail

Behavior

Seen traveling and foraging in noisy flocks of 5 to 30
or more birds, gleaning insects, eggs, and larvae from
shrubs and trees. Also visits feeders. These tiny incon-
spicuous, drab-colored birds may not be observed at all
until a group streams from a foraging site in a long,
continuous, undulating file. Roosts at night in a tight
mass of huddled bodies to conserve body heat. Calls
are given continuously by flocks, producing a buzzy,
excited chatter.

Habitat

Common in woodlands, parks, and residential areas.
Nest is an elaborate, gourd-shaped hanging structure
made of a number of materials and fastened to a tree
or shrub with spiderwebs.

Local Sites

Bushtits are found for the most part closer to the coast
or in the Puget Trough, though they have expanded
their range farther inland over previous decades.

FIELD NOTES The distinctive nests of Bushtits are often located
in residential areas, but use caution if observing one. If a pair is
disturbed either while making the nest or incubating eggs, they
may abandon both eggs and nest.

Year-round | Adult male

RED-BREASTED NUTHATCH

Sitta canadensis L 4½" (11 cm)

FIELD MARKS
Blue-gray upperparts;
rust-colored underparts

Black cap; white eyebrow; black
postocular stripe; white cheeks

Female and juvenile have duller
crown and paler underparts

Behavior
Climbs up and down trunks, small branches, and outer
twigs of trees, foraging for seeds, nuts, and insects.
Known to join mixed-species foraging flocks during
nonbreeding season and will often cache food. Male
feeds female during courtship; display consists of male
tilting side to side with head and tail upraised, back
feathers pricked up, and wings dropped. Pairs smear
pine pitch around nest entrance, presumably to ward
off predators. High-pitched, nasal call is a repeated *ink*.

Habitat
Found in coniferous and mixed woods, but nests exclusively in conifers. Winter range varies each year, as the
nuthatch is known to remain in its breeding range as
long as food is available.

Local Sites
Any of Washington and Oregon's coniferous forests are
likely to host breeding Red-breasteds in summer.

FIELD NOTES This small bird derives part of its name from its
resourceful method of obtaining food. It will often wedge a nut or
insect into a bark crevice, then pound it with its sharp, pointed
bill until it breaks through the respective shell or exoskeleton and
obtains the digestible parts within.

Year-round | Adult

WHITE-BREASTED NUTHATCH

Sitta carolinensis L 5¾" (15 cm)

FIELD MARKS

White face and breast; black cap

Blue-gray upperparts; wing and
tail feathers tipped in white

Rust or brown colored underparts
near legs

White pattern on blue-black tail

Behavior

Creeps down tree trunks or large branches in search
of insects or spiders. Will also gather nuts and seeds,
jam them into bark, and hammer or "hatch" the food
open with its bill. Visits backyard feeders, especially in
winter. Roosts in tree cavities, and sometimes even in
crevices of bark in summer. Song of the White-breasted
is typically a rapid series of nasal whistles in one pitch.
Call is a repeated, nasal *ern*.

Habitat

Almost exclusively in oaks west of the Cascades and
ponderosa pines on the east side of the Cascades. May
retreat to lower altitudes in order to avoid severe winter
storms. Builds nest in abandoned woodpecker holes or
in natural cavities inside decaying trees.

Local Sites

Oaks in southwest Oregon or pines east of the Cascades
are reliable for finding White-breasteds year-round, as
is Ridgefield National Wildlife Refuge in Washington.

FIELD NOTES In one of the more intriguing examples of tool use
in the bird world, this clever bird will smear the entrance to its
nest cavity with the remains of toxic insects, presumably in an
attempt to ward off potential predators.

Year-round | Adult

BROWN CREEPER

Certhia americana L 5¼" (13 cm)

FIELD MARKS
Mottled, streaky brown above

White eyebrow stripe

White underparts

Long, thin, decurved bill

Long, graduated tail

Behavior

Camouflaged by streaked brown plumage, creepers
spiral upward from the base of a tree, then fly to a
lower place on another tree in search of insects and
larvae in tree bark. A Brown Creeper will also eat fruit
and berries when insects are scarce. Its long, decurved
bill helps it to dig prey out of tree bark, its stiff tail
feathers serving as a prop against the trunk. Forages by
itself, in general, unless part of a mixed-species flock in
winter. Call is a soft, sibilant, almost inaudible *see*. Song
is a high-pitched *see-see-titi-see*, or a similar variation.

Habitat

Remains in forested areas, and builds nests behind
loose bark of dead or dying trees. May wander into
suburban and urban parks in winter.

Local Sites

The Brown Creeper can be difficult to spot, so listen for
its high-pitched call in forested regions of the Coast
Range, the Cascades, or the Blue Mountains.

FIELD NOTES If the creeper suspects the presence of a predator, it
will spread its wings and tail, press its body tight against the trunk
of a tree, and remain completely motionless. In this pose, its
camouflaged plumage makes it almost invisible.

Year-round | Adult

BEWICK'S WREN

Thryomanes bewickii L 5¼" (13 cm)

FIELD MARKS
Reddish brown or gray upperparts

Whitish underparts

Long, white eyebrow; long
decurved bill

Long rounded tail barred lightly
in black, edged in white

Behavior
The Bewick's Wren is often seen in pairs. Feeds
primarily on ground but also gleans insects and spiders
from vegetation. Holds tail high over back, flicking it
often from side to side. Male partially builds multiple
"dummy" nests, among which female chooses one to
complete. Throws head back to belt out its song, a
variable, high, thin, rising buzz, followed by a slow trill.
Calls include a flat, buzzy *jip*.

Habitat
Prefers brushland and open woods. Inquisitive and
tame, the Bewick's Wren can usually be found around
human habitation such as ranches and farms. Nests in
a variety of cavities from hollow logs to mailboxes.

Local Sites
The Bewick's Wren can be found on beaches and other
open areas close to the coast. It is also a
visitor to backyard feeding stations.

FIELD NOTES Another rather indistinct
bird of coastal Oregon is the Wrentit,
Chamaea fasciata (inset). Like the Bewick's, it
is either reddish brown or grayish above and
paler below, but it is set apart by its shorter,
stubby bill, pale iris, and lightly streaked breast.

Year-round | Adult

HOUSE WREN

Troglodytes aedon L 4¾" (12 cm)

FIELD MARKS
Grayish or brown upperparts

Fine black barring on wings
and tail

Pale gray underparts

Pale faint orbital ring, eyebrow

Thin, slightly decurved bill

Behavior
Noisy, conspicuous, and relatively tame, with a tail
often cocked upward. Gleans insects and spiders from
vegetation. While most species of wren forage low to
the ground, the House Wren will seek food at a variety
of levels, including high in the trees. Sings exuberantly
in a cascade of bubbling, whistled notes. Call is a rough
chek-chek, often running into a chatter.

Habitat
Inhabiting primarily open woodlands and thickets,
this bird is also tolerant of human presence, and can
be found in shrubbery around farms, parks, and urban
gardens. Nests in any cavity of suitable size.

Local Sites
Forest openings in much of Washington and Oregon,
particularly at lower elevations, provide suitable
nesting grounds for these birds in summer.

FIELD NOTES Commonly hidden in the reedy
marshes and cattail swamps of Washington
and Oregon, the Marsh Wren, *Cistothorus
palustris* (inset), reveals its location with its
constant, abrasive call of *tsuk-tsuk.* Like the
House Wren, it is brown overall, but has a
prominent white eye stripe and its mantle is
streaked black-and-white.

Year-round | Adult

WINTER WREN

Troglodytes troglodytes L 4" (10 cm)

FIELD MARKS
Short, stubby tail; stocky body

Dark reddish brown overall with
faint barring above

Heavily barred tail, flanks,
and underparts

Buff chin and throat

Behavior
Its rapid, cascading song belies the size of this small
songbird. Tends to be solitary when not paired for
breeding. An active ground feeder, it constantly bobs
its head and flicks its tail as it gleans insects and berries
from brush and dense thickets. Perches with its head
bobbing up and down as it sings a melodious series
of trills. Each male may employ up to 30 or more variations of his song. Call is a high, sharp *timp-timp*.

Habitat
Secretive inhabitant of dense brush in moist woods,
especially along stream banks. Nests with sticks, moss,
and grass in small cavities of hollowed-out logs or
beneath tree roots.

Local Sites
Winter Wrens can be found year-round in dense
coniferous and deciduous forests of the Coast Range,
Cascades, and Blue Mountains. In winter, they are
known to expand their range into lower elevations.

FIELD NOTES The Winter Wren is the only member of the family
Troglodytidae to have spread out from the New World by
crossing the Bering Strait from Alaska long ago. It now appears
throughout Asia, Europe, and northwestern Africa.

Year-round | Adult

AMERICAN DIPPER

Cinclus mexicanus L 7½" (19 cm)

FIELD MARKS

Sooty-gray overall

Short tail and wings

Straight dark bill

Pink legs and feet

Juvenile has paler, mottled underparts; pale bill

Behavior
Dippers are the only songbirds that swim. They use their wings to propel themselves sometimes 20 feet underwater, then walk on the river bottom to forage into crannies and under rocks for the larvae of various flies and mosquitoes. Also eat worms, water bugs, clams, snails, even small trout. In courtship, male will strut and sing with wings spread, after which both partners may jump up and bump breasts. Song is rattling and musical, loud enough to be heard over river's splash.

Habitat
Found along mountain streams fed by melting snow, glaciers, and rainfall. Descends to lower elevations in winter. Nests close to water level on cliffs, midstream boulders, bridges, or behind waterfalls.

Local Sites
Wilson River in the mountains east of Tillamook, Oregon, and Narada Falls in Mount Rainier National Park in Washington are both reliable spots for finding dippers.

FIELD NOTES The American Dipper has the uncanny ability to fly directly into and out of water. It may sometimes wade in from a river bank and dive from there, but it can also dive straight into water from a low flight.

Year-round | Adult

GOLDEN-CROWNED KINGLET

Regulus satrapa L 4" (10 cm)

FIELD MARKS
Yellow crown patch bordered in
black; tuft of orange feathers
within yellow on male

Olive green upperparts; pale
buff underparts

Broad whitish eyebrow; two
whitish wing bars

Behavior
Hovers on rapidly beating wings while foraging in the
foliage. Gleans insects, larvae, and seeds from bark and
leaves, reaching into tiny recesses with its short, straight
bill. Also drinks tree sap, sometimes following sapsuckers to fresh drill holes. Flits its wings while hopping on
branches. Song is almost inaudibly high, consisting of a
series of *tsee* notes accelerating into a trill. Call is a
high, thin *tsee tsee tsee*.

Habitat
Common in dense, coniferous woodlands. Nests fairly
high in conifer branches, constructing a spherical nest
of lichen, moss, bark, and feathers. Nest is so small that
eggs are laid one on top of the other.

Local Sites
Look high up in the trees of coniferous forests across
Washington and Oregon for this small, hardy species.

FIELD NOTES Most small species of songbirds that feed primarily
on insects migrate south to warmer climates when winter storms
tax their ability to keep up their energy with a depleted amount
of prey available. The Golden-crowned Kinglet, though, is
renowned for its ability to maintain normal body temperature
even in subfreezing conditions, enabling many birds to maintain
a range year-round in the mountains of Washington and Oregon.

Year-round | Adult male

RUBY-CROWNED KINGLET

Regulus calendula L 4¼" (11 cm)

FIELD MARKS

Olive green above; dusky below

Yellow-edged plumage on wings

Two white wing bars

Short black bill; white eye ring

Male's red crown patch seldom
visible except when agitated

Behavior

Often seen foraging in mixed-species flocks, the
Ruby-crowned Kinglet flicks its wings frequently as it
searches for insects and their eggs or larvae on tree
trunks, branches, and foliage. May also give chase to
flying insects or drink sap from tree wells drilled by
sapsuckers. Calls include a scolding *ji-dit;* song consists
of several high, thin *tsee* notes, followed by descending
tew notes, ending with a trilled three-note phrase.

Habitat

Common in coniferous and mixed woodlands, brushy
thickets, and backyard gardens. Hangs nest of moss,
lichen, twigs, and leaves from the branch of a tree.

Local Sites

Ruby-crowneds are very common in winter in lowlands west of the Cascades.

FIELD NOTES Though not closely related, the
Hutton's Vireo, *Vireo huttoni* (inset), looks uncannily
similar to the Ruby-crowned Kinglet. The two may
even be found in the same mixed-species foraging
flock. Look for the Hutton's thicker bill, larger size,
and its lack of a dark area beneath its lower wing
bar. Its song is a repeated *zu-wee, zu-wee,* which
can be heard year-round at coastal campgrounds.

Year-round | Adult male

WESTERN BLUEBIRD

Sialia mexicana L 7" (18 cm)

FIELD MARKS

Male has bright blue hood and upperparts; female blue-gray

Chestnut breast, flanks, and shoulders

Grayish white belly

Juvenile darkly marked overall

Behavior

Using its large, acute eyes, the bluebird hunts from a perch, then swoops down to seize crickets, grass-hoppers, and spiders, spotted from as far as 100 feet away. May also forage for earthworms or berries on the ground. Generally found in pairs or small family groups. More gregarious in winter, when many blue-birds will roost communally to keep up body tempera-ture. The call note of the Western Bluebird is a mellow *few,* extended in brief song to *few few fawee.*

Habitat

Found in woodlands, farmlands, orchards, and some residential areas. Both sexes build nests in holes in trees or posts as well as in nest boxes.

Local Sites

Though declining, Western Bluebirds can still be found year-round at sites such as Chehalem Mountain near Portland and Agate Reservoir near Medford, Oregon.

FIELD NOTES This small, brilliantly plumaged songbird has suffered a serious decline in population during the 20th century due to loss of habitat to development, and loss of nesting sites to introduced species such as the House Sparrow and the Euro-pean Starling. Nest box programs throughout Washington and Oregon are currently attempting to reverse this trend.

Year-round | Adult male

MOUNTAIN BLUEBIRD

Sialia currucoides L 7¼" (18 cm)

FIELD MARKS
Male is a bright sky blue overall, paler below

Female is dusky blue-gray overall, sometimes washed with rusty orange on the breast

Longer-winged than Western Bluebird

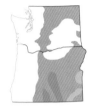

Behavior
Generally seen alone, in a pair, or in a small family group. Hunts from a perch for flying insects, caterpillars, and grasshoppers. Also known to hover over grasslands while searching for prey. May forage on the ground for fruit and berries, particularly in winter. Though not the most vocal bird, its call is a thin *few*. Song is a series of low, warbled *tru-lee*s.

Habitat
Found in open woodlands, agricultural areas, and grasslands generally at fairly high elevations. Nests in tree cavities or nest boxes. Highly migratory, tends to abandon higher elevations as winter progresses.

Local Sites
Two good spots to find this species are Sagehen Rest Area west of Burns, Oregon, and Umtanum Road heading out of Ellensburg, Washington.

FIELD NOTES Though it inhabits many of the same montane areas, the Townsend's Solitaire, *Myadestes townsendi* (inset), is hard to confuse with a bluebird. It is drab gray with a black tail, blackish flight feathers, and buffy wing patches that show in flight. Its continuous, prolonged song is also distinctive. It is generally found in high-elevation coniferous forests east of the Cascades.

Year-round | Adult

SWAINSON'S THRUSH

Catharus ustulatus L 7" (18 cm)

FIELD MARKS
Brownish above, paler below

Buffy breast with dark spots

Buffy lores and cheeks; bold,
buffy eye ring

Black bill with pinkish base
on lower mandible

Behavior
Sits still when not foraging, so can be difficult to spot
with its drab brown plumage. Forages through leaf
litter for insects, snails, and earthworms, but may also
glean food off the leaves of trees or catch some insects
in flight. Known to vibrate its feet on soil in order to
stir invertebrates out of hiding. Song is an ascending
spiral of varied whistles. Common call is a liquid *whit*.
During migration, listen at night for a clear *queep*.

Habitat
Common in mid- to low-elevation moist woodlands.
Nests close to ground, usually on branch of a conifer.
Migrates by night to wintering grounds in Mexico.

Local Sites
One of the region's most abundant breeders, look for
it in the undergrowth of forests on the eastern and
western slopes of the Cascades.

FIELD NOTES The similarly plumaged Hermit Thrush,
Catharus guttatus (inset), has variably colored
upperparts, depending on which subspecies is
encountered. Found in coniferous and mixed
woodlands, this bird can be distinguished from the
Swainson's by its reddish tail, white eye ring, and
chup call note.

Year-round | Adults

AMERICAN ROBIN

Turdus migratorius L 10" (25 cm)

FIELD MARKS

Brick red underparts, paler in
female, spotted in juvenile

Brownish gray above with darker
head and tail

White throat and lower belly

Broken white eye ring; yellow bill

Behavior

Best known and largest of the thrushes, often seen on
suburban lawns, hopping about and cocking its head
in search of earthworms. The American Robin gleans
butterflies, damselflies, and other flying insects from
foliage and sometimes takes prey in flight. Robins also
eat fruit, especially in fall and winter. This broad plant
and animal diet makes them one of the most successful
and wide-ranging thrushes. Calls include a rapid *tut-
tut-tut*; song is a variable *cheerily cheer-up cheerio*.

Habitat

Common and widespread, the American Robin forages
on lawns and in woodlands. Nests in shrubs, trees, and
even on sheltered windowsills. Winters in moist woodlands, suburbs, and parks.

Local Sites

Look for robins year-round almost anywhere in Washington and Oregon, including the nearest backyard.
This adaptable bird thrives in residential, agricultural,
and natural habitats.

FIELD NOTES The juvenile robin, which can be seen every year
between May and September, has a paler breast, like the female
of the species, but its underparts are heavily spotted with brown.
Look as well for the buff fringes on its back and wing feathers
and its short, pale buff eyebrow.

Year-round | Adult male

VARIED THRUSH

Ixoreus naevius L 9½" (24 cm)

FIELD MARKS
Blue-gray upperparts; orange
breast, throat, eyebrows, and
wing bars

Male has dark blue-black ear
coverts and breast band; female's
are brownish gray

White undertail coverts

Behavior

Forages on the ground or low in undergrowth for
insects, caterpillars, berries, and acorns. Generally seen
by itself or in a pair, except in winter when flocks may
occur. Tends to stay hidden in shadows, obscuring
its striking plumage. Courtship display involves tail-
cocking and bowing that accentuates these birds' richly
designed wing patterns. Song is a slow series of variably
pitched, prolonged notes. Call is a soft, low *tschook*.

Habitat

Found in dense, moist woodlands, especially coniferous
forests, but also visits backyard feeders. Female builds
nest not far from ground on branch or fork of a tree.

Local Sites

Listen for the male Varied's eerily pitched song in
summer in damp coniferous forests of the Coast
Ranges and the Cascades.

FIELD NOTES When its plumage is obscured within its preferred
habitat of damp, dark woodlands, this bird structurally resembles
its close relative, the American Robin, yet it is not nearly as gregarious or conspicuous. In fact, there is much still to be learned
about this secretive species. Ornithologists have not yet come to
fully undertand either their mating system or their short-distance
migration patterns.

Summer | Adult

EUROPEAN STARLING

Sturnus vulgaris L 8½" (22 cm)

FIELD MARKS
Head iridescent black when breeding; speckled wth white in fall

Buffy tips on back, tail feathers

Yellow bill; base in summer pale blue on male, pink on female

Behavior
A social and aggressive bird, the European Starling feeds on a tremendous variety of food, ranging from invertebrates—such as snails, worms, and spiders—to fruits, berries, grains, seeds, and garbage. It probes ground for food, opening its bill to create small holes and expose prey. Usually seen in flocks, except during nesting season. Imitates calls of other species, especially grackles, and emits high-pitched notes, including squeaks, hisses, chirps, and twittering.

Habitat
The adaptable starling thrives in a variety of habitats near humans, from urban centers to agricultural regions. Nests in cavities, ranging from crevices in urban settings to woodpecker holes and nest boxes.

Local Sites
Widespread year-round throughout much of Washington and Oregon, the starling is likely to be found in most local parks.

FIELD NOTES A Eurasian species introduced into New York's Central Park in 1890, the European Starling has since spread throughout the U.S. and Canada. Abundant, bold, and aggressive, starlings often compete for and take over nest sites of native birds, including bluebirds, Wood Ducks, a variety of woodpeckers, Tree Swallows, and Purple Martins.

Year-round | Adult

CEDAR WAXWING

Bombycilla cedrorum L 7¼" (18 cm)

FIELD MARKS

Distinctive sleek crest

Black mask bordered in white

Brownish head, back, breast, and sides; pale yellow belly; gray rump

Yellow terminal tail band

May have red, waxy tips on wings

Behavior

Eats the most fruit of any North American bird. Up to 84 percent of its diet is made up of a variety of berries and other small fruits. Also eats sap, flower petals, and insects. Cedar Waxwings are gregarious in nature and band together for foraging and protection. Flocks containing several to a few hundred birds may feed side by side in winter, then rapidly disperse, startling potential predators. Call is a thin, high-pitched *zeee*.

Habitat

Found in open habitats wherever berries are available. Abundance and location of berries influence this bird's migration patterns: It moves long distances only when food sources run out.

Local Sites

Found throughout Washington and Oregon, wherever fruit-bearing trees are plentiful.

FIELD NOTES The only other North American member of the Bombycillidae family is the Bohemian Waxwing, *Bombycilla garrulus* (inset). Larger and grayer than the Cedar, its wings are intricately marked in white, black, red, and yellow. Look for flocks between December and February wherever fruit-bearing trees occur in eastern Washington and Oregon.

Year-round | Adult

ORANGE-CROWNED WARBLER

Vermivora celata L 5" (13 cm)

FIELD MARKS

Olive-green above, pale yellow-green below; brightest yellow on undertail coverts

Dark eyeline, faint yellow eyebrow

Orange crown patch is absent on some females and indiscernible on some males

Behavior

Often seen by itself, deliberately foraging low in trees, shrubs, and grasses for insects. Probes into leaf litter for food as well. Also feeds occassionally on flower nectar, fruits, and the sap of sapsuckers' drill holes. Known to respond readily to pishing by birders. Song is a high-pitched staccato trill that slows and drops pitch slightly at the end. Call note is a sharp *chip*. Listen as well for this bird's flight call, a high, clear *seet*.

Habitat

Inhabits open, brushy woodlands, forest edges, and thickets. Sometimes found in suburban areas. Nests on the ground among shrubs or grasses.

Local Sites

Most abundant on the western slope of the Cascades, the Orange-crowned Warbler can also be found in migration throughout Washington and Oregon.

FIELD NOTES The Orange-crowned Warbler winters as far north as the southern portions of the United States, considerably farther north than most members of the Parulidae family. This is perhaps due to its habit of investigating leaf litter for food. Other wood-warblers, dependent on fresh foliage to attract the insects on which they feed, must head to Central and South America to maintain a steady source of prey.

Year-round | Adult male

YELLOW WARBLER

Dendroica petechia L 5" (13 cm)

FIELD MARKS
Bright yellow overall

Plump and short-tailed

Dark eye prominent in yellow face

Male shows distinct reddish streaks below; streaks faint or absent in female

Behavior
Forages in trees, shrubs, and bushes, gleaning insects, larvae, and fruit from branches and leaves. Will sometimes spot flying insects from a perch and chase them down. Mostly seen by itself or in a pair. Male and female both feed nestlings. Yellow warblers habitually bob their tails and are quite vocal. Song is a rapid, variable *sweet-sweet-I'm-so-sweet.*

Habitat
Favors wet habitats, especially those with willows and alders, but also lives in open woodlands, gardens, and orchards. Nests in the forks of trees or bushes at eye level or a little higher.

Local Sites
The Yellow Warbler breeds in open woodlands throughout much of Washington and Oregon. Good spots to find one are Malheur National Wildlife Refuge and Fern Ridge Reservoir, both in Oregon.

FIELD NOTES Another small, largely yellow warbler inhabiting moist woodlands of Washington and Oregon is the Wilson's Warbler, *Wilsonia pusilla* (inset: male, left; female, right). It is a darker olive-green above than the Yellow Warbler and the male sports a black cap. Neither sex shows any streaking on the underparts. Wilson's Warblers are primarily found west of the Cascades, anywhere in migration.

Breeding | Adult male "Audubon's"

YELLOW-RUMPED WARBLER

Dendroica coronata L 5½" (14 cm)

FIELD MARKS

Bright yellow rump; yellow patch
on sides of breast; yellow throat

Winter birds grayish brown above;
white below with brown streaking

Breeding males have yellow patch
on crown; grayish blue upperparts; black breast patch

Behavior
Perhaps the most abundant warbler in Washington and
Oregon, darts about branches from tree to tree or in
bushes, foraging for myrtle berries and seeds. Often
seen in winter in small foraging flocks. Will switch to
primarily insect and spider diet before spring migration. Sings soft, repeated *seedle,* fading at end. Call a
low *chup,* with rising intonation.

Habitat
Found in brushy and wooded habitats, especially at
field edges. Seeks out areas rich in bayberry or juniper
thickets. Female builds cup-shaped nest of bark, twigs,
and roots in conifer trees.

Local Sites
The Yellow-rumped Warbler can be found breeding in
most conifer forests of Washington and Oregon, except
those below sea level.

FIELD NOTES The eastern subspecies group of the
Yellow-rumped Warbler, referred to as the "Myrtle Warbler" (inset: male), was once thought to be
a separate species. It is a winter visitor to coastal
Washington and Oregon and a migrant throughout.
It is similar to "Audubon's" but has a white throat and
white eyebrow.

Year-round | Adult male

BLACK-THROATED GRAY WARBLER

Dendroica nigrescens L 5" (13 cm)

FIELD MARKS
Black-and-white striped head

Small yellow spot in front of eye

Gray back streaked with black

White underparts and undertail
coverts; flanks streaked
with black

Behavior
Gleans insects, larvae, and caterpillars from low- to
mid-level branches, twigs, and leaves. Seen singly or
in a pair through breeding season, this bird may join
small flocks prior to fall migration. Sings even as it forages for insects. Varied songs include a buzzy *weezy
weezy weezy weezy-weet,* with the ultimate or penulti-
mate note higher. Call is a flat *tip.*

Habitat
Inhabits a variety of lowland woodlands, brushlands,
and chaparral. Female builds nest of plant material,
grasses, and weeds in forks or branches of trees, fairly
close to the ground.

Local Sites
Among the the earliest spring migrants to appear in
Washington and Oregon, look for Black-throated Gray
Warblers as early as April in wooded areas in the
foothills and valleys west of the Cascades.

FIELD NOTES The female Black-throated Gray-
Warbler (inset) is similar to the male, but still dis-
tinguishable in the field. Look for her white chin
and throat, where the male has black plumage,
and look for a gray crown streaked with black,
instead of the all-black crown of the male.

Year-round | Adult male

TOWNSEND'S WARBLER

Dendroica townsendi L 5" (13 cm)

FIELD MARKS

Head boldly marked yellow and black on male, yellow and olive-green on female

Black streaking on flanks and on olive-green mantle

Yellow breast; white belly

Behavior

Forages high up in mature conifers for insects, caterpillars, and spiders. In general, aggressive toward other species, but may join mixed foraging flocks after breeding. Known to hybridize with closely related Hermit Warbler, producing an offspring of mixed characteristics dubbed the "Heto Warbler." Song is variable but consists of a series of hoarse *zee* notes rising in pitch and dropping at end. Call is a sharp *tsik*.

Habitat

Common in coniferous and mixed forests. Both sexes build nest of bark, grasses, and other materials high up on a limb of a mature conifer.

Local Sites

Coastal campgrounds in Oregon are good places to find Townsend's in winter. Scan high up in the trees of the Cascades and Blue Mountains to find a breeding pair in summer.

FIELD NOTES The Hermit Warbler, *Dendroica occidentalis* (inset: male, left; female, right), is a common breeder in montane conifer forests of Washington and Oregon. It is set apart from the Townsend's by yellow cheeks, white underparts, and gray upperparts. A more difficult identification is the hybrid offspring between the two, which shows intermediate characteristics such as a yellowish streaked breast, an olive-green mantle, and bright yellow cheeks.

Year-round | Adult male

COMMON YELLOWTHROAT

Geothlypis trichas L 5" (13 cm)

FIELD MARKS

Adult male shows broad, black mask bordered above by light gray

Female lacks black mask, has whitish patch around eyes

Grayish olive upperparts; bright yellow throat and breast; pale yellow undertail coverts

Behavior
This widespread warbler generally remains close to the ground, skulking and hiding in undergrowth. May also be seen climbing vertically on stems and singing from exposed perches. While foraging, cocks tail and hops on ground to glean insects, caterpillars, and spiders from foliage, twigs, and reeds. Sometimes feeds while hovering, or gives chase to flying insects. One version of variable song is a loud, rolling *wichity-wichity-wich.* Calls include a raspy *chuck.*

Habitat
Stays low in marshes, shrubby fields, woodland edges, and thickets near water. Nests atop piles of weeds and grass, or in small shrubs.

Local Sites
Found in summer in wet habitats mostly west of the Cascades. Reliable spots include Malheur National Wildlife Refuge and Fern Ridge Reservoir in Oregon and Nisqually National Wildlife Refuge in Washington.

FIELD NOTES The colors of the Common Yellowthroat vary considerably among subspecies separated by geography. Differences include the quality of yellow on the underparts, the extent of olive shading on the upperparts, and the width and color of the border between the male's mask and crown, which can range from stark white to gray.

Breeding | Adult male

WESTERN TANAGER

Piranga ludoviciana L 7¼" (18 cm)

FIELD MARKS
Bright red hood on breeding male

Yellow underparts, nape, and
rump; yellow-green face on female

Black wings and tail

Upper wing bar is yellow, lower
wing bar is white

Behavior
Forages both in trees and on ground for insects, especially wasps and bees, and for fruit. May join mixed-species foraging flocks after breeding. Known to visit birdbaths, but rarely feeders. Both sexes are known to sing a hoarse three-to-five-phrase series of repeated *chu-wee* notes, somewhat resembling American Robin or Black-headed Grosbeak. Call is a quick, slurred rattle: *pit-ick*, *pit-er-ick*, or *tu-weep*.

Habitat
Found in coniferous and pine-oak forests. Cup-shaped nest is located far out on branches.

Local Sites
This stunning bird can be found in spring and summer in forests throughout much of Washington and Oregon. May also appear in any number of habitats during migration, including suburban areas.

FIELD NOTES During fall migration, look for a male who has already begun molting from bright red to yellow on his face. He can still be distinguished from the female by his black mantle and thicker wing bars. The female is in general a drabber yellow overall, but some may show a gray belly and chin and a white upper wing bar.

Year-round | Adult male

SPOTTED TOWHEE

Pipilo maculatus L 7½" (19 cm)

FIELD MARKS

Black upperparts and hood on male; gray-brown on female

Rufous flanks and white underparts; white spots on back and scapulars; two white wing bars;

Long tail with white corners

Behavior

This species employs the distinctive double-scratch technique—kicking its feet backward in the leaf litter, head held low and tail pointed up, attempting to expose seeds, fruit, and small arthropods, especially beetles, caterpillars, and spiders. Generally seen singly or in a pair, but family groups may stay togeather for a short time after nesting. Sings a simple trill of variable speed from an exposed perch, though geograpahical variations occur. Call is an upslurred, inquisitive *queee*.

Habitat

Common in chaparral, brushy thickets, and forest edges. Nests on ground, and occasionally in low trees or shrubs. Known to visit backyards where seed is scattered on the ground.

Local Sites

A widespread breeder throughout much of Washington and Oregon, the Spotted Towhee is found in winter in brushy habitats mostly west of the Cascades.

FIELD NOTES If threatened at the nest, the female Spotted Towhee will tuck in its wings, prick up its tail, and sprint away at an even speed, in this way closely resembling a chipmunk or other small rodent. This "rodent run" display is used to lure nest predators away from the eggs, whose presence would be revealed if the incubating bird were to simply fly away.

Breeding | Adult

CHIPPING SPARROW

Spizella passerina L 5½" (14 cm)

FIELD MARKS

Breeding adult shows bright chestnut crown; white eyebrow; gray cheek and nape

Winter adult has streaked brown crown and a brown face

Streaked brown wings and back, unstreaked gray breast and belly

Behavior
Forages on the ground for insects, caterpillars, spiders, and seeds. Found singly, in a pair, or in a small family group after nesting. Sings from high perch a one-pitched, rapid-fire trill of dry *chip* notes. Call in flight or when foraging is a high, hard *seep* or *tsik*.

Habitat
The Chipping Sparrow can be found in suburban lawns and gardens, woodland edges, and pine and oak forests. Tends to remain in more open wooded areas. Nests close to the ground in branches or vine tangles.

Local Sites
Seen primarily in open woodlands of eastern Washington and Oregon, Chipping Sparrows are especially abundant in the Blue Mountains.

FIELD NOTES Because the Savannah Sparrow, *Passerculus sandwichensis* (inset), has few markings that distinctively set it off from the Chipping Sparrow and similar species, a combination of plumage, habitat, and behavior must be considered to make a definite identification. Staying primarily on the ground in fields or roadsides, the Savannah breeds throughout Washington and Oregon and is resident along the coast. It is much less secretive than many other similarly streaked sparrows. Look for its notched tail and its broad whitish eyebrow, usually yellowish in front of the eyes.

Year-round | Adult "Slate-colored"

FOX SPARROW

Passerella iliaca L 7" (18 cm)

FIELD MARKS

Slate gray or dark brown crown
and back

Dull rufous wings and tail

White underparts heavily marked
with triangular spots that converge on breast and form streaks
on flanks

Behavior

Forages by double-scratching leaf litter like towhees
in order to expose seeds, fruits, berries, insects, spiders,
and snails. Generally seen singly or in a pair in spring
and summer; in small flocks in winter and during
migration. Males sing a variety of songs, generally
buzzy or trilled. Call is a sharp *tchewp*.

Habitat

Found in montane coniferous and deciduous woodlands, chaparral, and riparian areas. Nests on the
ground or in a low shrub.

Local Sites

Coastal thickets, such as those at Juanita Bay Park in
Washington, are good spots to search for Fox Sparrows
in winter. Find breeding birds in high-elevation forests
of the Cascades and Blue Mountains.

FIELD NOTES As many as 18 recognized subspecies of the Fox
Sparrow occur in North America. These subspecies are broken
down into four main groups of which the slate-colored (opposite)
is the most widespread in the Pacific Northwest. Look as well for
the sooty group, common west of the Cascades in winter, with a
dark brown back that contrasts less with wings and tail. The
thick-billed group occurs in the Klamath Basin of Oregon and is
marked by thinner breast streaking and a larger bill. Members of
the red group, with bright red breast streaking, are rare vagrants.

Year-round | Adult

SONG SPARROW

Melospiza melodia L 5¾" (16 cm)

FIELD MARKS
Underparts whitish, with streaks on sides and breast that converge into a dark breast spot

Streaked brown and gray above; broad, grayish eyebrow; broad, dark malar stripe

Long, rounded tail

Behavior
Forages in trees and bushes and on ground for larvae, fruits, and berries, sometimes scratching ground to unearth grain or insects. Coastal birds take mollusks and crustaceans as well. Perches in the open, belting out its melodious song, three to four short, clear notes followed by a buzzy *tow-wee* and a trill. Female broods young while male defends territory intently, singing from exposed perch and battling competitors.

Habitat
Common in suburban and rural gardens, weedy fields, dense streamside thickets, and forest edges. Nests on the ground or near it in trees and bushes.

Local Sites
A widespread and common species throughout Washington and Oregon; listen at dawn and dusk in the nearest brushy park for this bird's conspicuous song.

FIELD NOTES Occurring across most of North America, from the Aleutian Islands of Alaska to the borders of Mexico and eastward along the Atlantic Coast, there are over 30 recognized subspecies of Song Sparrow, all of which have adapted to various specific environments. Pale races inhabit arid regions in the Southwest; darker races inhabit more humid regions; and larger races inhabit oceanic islands. In Washington and Oregon, birds west of the Cascades are noticeably darker plumaged.

Winter | Adult

GOLDEN-CROWNED SPARROW

Zonotrichia atricapilla L 7" (18 cm)

FIELD MARKS

Dull golden crown patch bordered in black; mostly gray face

Streaked brown upperparts; dull gray underparts; flanks washed with brown

Golden crown patch obscured in immatures

Behavior
Forages on the ground and in low foliage for seeds and insects. Also known to consume flower petals, buds, and some fruits and berries. Will double-scratch like a towhee when foraging. Forms flocks with other species in winter; often found in the company of its close relative, the White-crowned Sparrow. Song is a descending series of three or more plaintive, whistled notes, *oh dear me*. Flight call is a soft *tseep*. Also emits a loud, clear *tsick*.

Habitat
Common in winter in lowland brushy areas, parks, and suburban areas. Known to frequent backyard feeders. Found in more montane regions during migration.

Local Sites
Almost any brush pile in the western interior valleys between the Cascades and the Coast Ranges of Washington and Oregon are likely to have a couple of singing Golden-crowneds.

FIELD NOTES A flock of Golden-crowned Sparrows, even when not singing or calling, can be detected audibly by their habit of scratching through leaf litter to expose food. Getting a good view of this species, though, can be a little more difficult. Try producing a *pish* sound yourself, a technique which can often bring the bird right to you.

Year-round | Adult *pugetensis*

WHITE-CROWNED SPARROW

Zonotrichia leucophrys L 7" (18 cm)

FIELD MARKS

Black-and-white striped crown

Underparts gray; flanks washed with brown

Brownish upperparts with blackish brown streaking

Pink, orange, or yellowish bill

Behavior

Scratches the ground in order to expose insects, caterpillars, and seeds. Also gleans food from vegetation. Male sings from exposed perches to announce territory, sometimes inciting fights, and to attract females. Song variable by region and often heard in winter. Usually one or more thin, whistled notes followed by a twittering trill. Calls include a loud *pink* and a sharp *tseep*.

Habitat

Found in natural and suburban woodlands, thickets, and brushy areas. Nests close to ground.

Local Sites

Look for the *pugetensis* subspecies of White-crowned Sparrow, with yellow bill and gray lores, west of the Cascades and around Puget Sound; for the *gambelii* subspecies, with orange bill, in winter throughout the region; and for the *oriantha* subspecies, with pink bill and black lores, in summer in the Blue Mountains.

FIELD NOTES The similarly plumaged White-throated Sparrow, *Zonotrichia albicollis* (inset: tan-striped morph, top; white-striped morph, bottom), is an uncommon fall and winter visitor to regions west of the Cascades. It is set apart from the White-crowned by its spot of yellow in front of the eyes and its sharply outlined white throat.

Year-round | Adult male "Oregon"

DARK-EYED JUNCO

Junco hyemalis L 6¼" (16 cm)

FIELD MARKS
Black hood on male, dark brown on female

Reddish brown back; gray rump

White belly and undertail coverts

White outer tail feathers in flight

Juveniles are heavily streaked

Behavior
Scratches on ground and forages by gleaning seeds, grain, berries, insects, caterpillars, and fruit from plants. Forms flocks in winter, when adult males may remain farther north or at greater elevations than immatures and females. Song is a short, musical trill that varies in pitch and tempo. Calls include a sharp *dit*, and a rapid twittering in flight.

Habitat
Winters in a wide variety of habitats, especially patchy wooded areas. Breeds in coniferous or mixed woodlands. Nests on or close to ground.

Local Sites
One of the region's most abundant species, look for Dark-eyed Juncos in natural areas, city parks, and at backyard feeding stations.

FIELD NOTES The various subspecies of the Dark-eyed Junco were unified into one species in 1973, although they are widely scattered geographically and fairly disparate in their field marks. In Washington and Oregon, easily the dominant subspecies is the "Oregon" (opposite), but keep an eye out as well between October and April for the "Slate-colored" (inset: male), with uniform gray hood, breast, flanks, back, and rump.

Breeding | Adult male

BLACK-HEADED GROSBEAK

Pheucticus melanocephalus L 8¼" (21 cm)

FIELD MARKS

Male has cinnamon underparts and nape; black head and upperparts; two prominent wing bars

Female buffy overall, with streaked mantle

Yellow wing linings show in flight; large, dark, triangular bill

Behavior
Forages for seeds, insects, caterpillars, berries, and fruit on the ground and in trees and bushes. In Washington and Oregon, generally seen singly or in a pair. Nestlings are brooded by both male and female. Song is a rich, whistled warble. Very soft songs may also be emitted by either sex while incubating eggs. Call is a sharp *eek*.

Habitat
Inhabits open and streamside woodlands and forest edges. Known to visit backyard feeders and suburban parks. Nests moderately high up in dense vegetation of trees or shrubs, usually near water.

Local Sites
In summer, listen for the Black-headed's melodious song in deciduous forests throughout Washington and Oregon, especially in riparian areas.

FIELD NOTES The Black-headed Grosbeak will hybridize with its cousin, the Rose-breasted Grosbeak, *Pheucticus ludovicianus*, where their ranges overlap in the Great Plains. Their nearly identical songs no doubt promote the interchange. Hybrids may occasionally occur at feeders in Washington and Oregon. They are marked by underparts mottled in red, orange, and white and by a dusky orange and black head pattern.

Year-round | Adult male

LAZULI BUNTING

Passerina amoena L 5½" (14 cm)

FIELD MARKS

Male has bright blue hood and upperparts; cinnamon upper breast; white belly and undertail coverts; two white wing bars

Female drab brown overall, with bluish rump and tail; whitish belly; two faint buffy wing bars

Behavior

Forages on ground and in low foliage primarily for seeds. May also consume insects and caterpillars. Generally seen singly or in a pair, but may join small flocks after breeding and larger flocks during migration, sometimes with other species of buntings or sparrows. Persistently sings a vivacious series of varied phrases, sometimes with repeated notes. Highly territorial, many young males learn songs not from parents, but from competing males. Call is a short *pik*.

Habitat

Found in a variety of low-elevation brushy habitats, especially on hillsides, in valleys, and along streams. Nests close to ground in small bush or tree.

Local Sites

Most widespread east of the Cascades. Scan along riparian areas in summer in Owyhee Valley in Oregon and Hardy Canyon or Kent Ponds in Washington for this brilliantly plumaged bird.

FIELD NOTES The female Lazuli Bunting (inset) has drab brown plumage overall in stark contrast to the male's sky blue hood and back. At first glance, she can be mistaken for a sparrow, but note her unstreaked back, warm buffy breast, and the blue tint to her rump, tail coverts, and to a lesser extent her wing coverts.

Year-round | Adult male

RED-WINGED BLACKBIRD

Agelaius phoeniceus L 8¾" (22 cm)

FIELD MARKS

Male is glossy black; bright red shoulder patches broadly edged in buffy yellow below

Females densely streaked overall

Pointed black bill

Wings slightly rounded at tips

Behavior
Runs and hops while foraging for insects, seeds, and grains in pastures and open fields. The male's bright red shoulder patches are usually visible when it sings from a perch, often atop a cattail or tall weed stalk, defending its territory. At other times only the yellow border may be visible. Territorially aggressive, a male's social status is dependent on the amount of red he displays on his shoulders. Song is a liquid, gurgling *konk-la-reee*, ending in a trill. Call is a low *chack* note.

Habitat
Breeds in colonies, mainly in freshwater marshes and wet fields with thick vegetation. Nests in cattails, bushes, or dense grass near water. During winter, large flocks forage in wooded swamps and farm fields.

Local Sites
The Red-winged Blackbird is a widespread and abundant breeder in wetlands throughout Washington and Oregon. It can be found almost anywhere except dense forests and tall peaks.

FIELD NOTES Usually less visible within large flocks of singing males, the female Red-winged (inset) is streaked dark brown above and has dusky white underparts heavily streaked with dark brown. In winter you may find a whole flock of only females.

Year-round | Adult

WESTERN MEADOWLARK

Sturnella neglecta L 9½" (24 cm)

FIELD MARKS
Black V-shaped breast band
on yellow underparts

Long, pointed bill

Brown and white crown stripes;
black and brown barred back

Heavily streaked white flanks

Behavior
A ground feeder with strong legs for walking; forages
through marsh edges, lakeshores, fields, meadows, and
lawns, gleaning whatever might be available. Uses long,
thin, sharp-tipped bill to probe deep into soil and
pluck out a variety of food including seeds, fruit,
insects and worms. Found by itself or in a pair during
breeding season, but highly gregarious at other times
of year. Sings from exposed perch a series of bubbling,
melodious notes of variable length, usually accelerating
toward the end. Gives a sharp *chuck* note on the ground
and a whistled *wheet* call in flight.

Habitat
Prefers the open space offered by pastures, grasslands,
and farm fields. Nests on the ground by creating a
dome or partial dome of grass and weeds. Often uses
fence posts and utility wires as perches.

Local Sites
A year-round resident of much of Washington and
Oregon, large flocks often gather and perch on fence
posts near roadsides, especially in winter.

FIELD NOTES The Western Meadowlark was elected state bird of
Oregon in 1927 following a statewide poll of schoolchildren con-
ducted by the Oregon Audubon Society.

Breeding | Adult male

YELLOW-HEADED BLACKBIRD

Xanthocephalus xanthocephalus L 9½" (24 cm)

FIELD MARKS

Male has prominent yellow hood and breast; black body and lores; large white wing patch

Female is washed with yellow on her face and breast; dark brown body and crown

Stubby, black, triangular bill

Behavior

Highly gregarious, the Yellow-headed Blackbird breeds in colonies and forms large flocks outside of the breeding season, sometimes numbering in the thousands. Forages communally on ground for insects, larvae, snails, grain, and seeds. Highly territorial, the Yellow-headed will attack other birds and even humans who intrude on its territory. Unmusical, raspy song begins with a few loud, harsh notes and ends in a long, descending buzz resembling the sound of a chainsaw. Call note is a hoarse croak.

Habitat

Found at freshwater bodies of water such as marshes, reedy lakes, and cattail swamps. Nests among grasses and reeds just above the water's surface.

Local Sites

Malheur, Klamath, Ridgefield, and Columbia National Wildlife Refuges all host breeding colonies of Yellow-headed Blackbirds in summer.

FIELD NOTES The female Yellow-headed weaves her nest of sedges and grass in emergent vegetation in or near water. She seems to intentionally use wet materials in the construction of her nest, and as the wet vegetation dries, it shrinks and tightens the weave into a very sturdy structure.

Year-round | Adult male

BREWER'S BLACKBIRD

Euphagus cyanocephalus L 9" (23 cm)

FIELD MARKS

Male is black with purplish gloss on head and neck; greenish gloss on body and wings; less glossy in winter

Male has yellow eyes; female has brown eyes, gray-brown body

Bill is sharp and straight

Behavior

Like all blackbirds, the Brewer's has strong legs and feet that allow it to walk for long stretches as it forages on the ground. With straight, strong, sharp-tipped bill, it eats insects, fruit, grain, and seeds. Raises tail and inclines body while foraging. Will assemble in parking lots to pick protein-rich insects from car grilles and to scavenge handouts. Spreads tail and droops wings as it sings its short, raucous, wheezy *quee-ee* or *k-seee*. Call is a harsh *check*.

Habitat

Common in open habitats, including fields, marshes, suburbs with parks, and parking lots. Breeds away from cities in agricultural areas or grasslands. Female builds coarse, cup-shaped nest of needles, grasses, and twigs. She pads inside of cup with either mud or cow manure.

Local Sites

Check the nearest supermarket parking lot for this ubiquitous year-round resident of much of Washington and Oregon.

FIELD NOTES Strong jaw musculature allows blackbirds to close their bills —and then forcefully open them in an action called "gaping." Gaping allows the birds to pry into crevices, soft bark, dirt, and leaf litter to expose prey unavailable to other birds.

Year-round | Adult male

BROWN-HEADED COWBIRD

Molothrus ater L 7½" (19 cm)

FIELD MARKS

Male's brown head contrasts with metallic black body

Female gray-brown above, paler below with a whitish throat

Short, dark, pointed bill

Juvenile streaked below

Behavior
Often forages on the ground among herds of cattle, feeding on insects flushed by the grazing farm animals. Also feeds heavily on grass seeds and agricultural grain, and is sometimes viewed as a threat to crops. Generally cocks its tail up while feeding. The Brown-headed Cowbird is a nest parasite and lays its eggs in the nests of other species, leaving the responsibilities of feeding and fledging of young to the host birds. Song is a squeaky gurgling. Calls includes a squeaky whistle and a harsh rattle.

Habitat
Cowbirds prefer open habitat such as farmlands, pastures, prairies, and edgelands bordering forests. Also found in general around human habitation.

Local Sites
With the fragmentation of woodlands and the clearing of land for development, this cowbird has extended its breeding range throughout Washington and Oregon.

FIELD NOTES The Brown-headed Cowbird flourishes throughout North America, adapting to newly cleared lands and exposing new songbirds—now more than 200 species—to its parasitic egg-laying habit. The female Brown-headed Cowbird lays up to 40 eggs a season in the nests of host birds, leaving the task of raising her young to the host species.

Year-round | Adult male

BULLOCK'S ORIOLE

Icterus bullockii L 8¼" (22 cm)

FIELD MARKS

Male has bold orange face and underparts; black crown, back, tail, throat patch, and eye line

Female has yellow face, throat, and breast; drab olive wings, back, and tail; grayish belly

Large white wing patches

Behavior

Forages in trees and bushes for insects, berries, and fruit. Probes into crevices with long, sharply pointed bill for ants, mayflies, and spiders. During courtship, male chases female and displays with wing-drooping and repeated bowing. Pairs are noisy and conspicuous, and spend much time together, but mate for only one season. Song is variable, but always composed of whistles and harsher notes; call is a clear, harsh *cheh*, sometimes given in a series.

Habitat

Breeds in open wooded areas, especially those rife with deciduous trees. Female weaves grasses into intricate hanging baskets or pouches for use as nests.

Local Sites

Breeds mainly east of the Cascades; look for the Bullock's in lowland streamside areas, such as those found in the Klamath Basin of Oregon and Potholes State Park in Washington.

FIELD NOTES The Bullock's Oriole was once considered the same species as the Baltimore Oriole, which is a rare migrant to the Pacific Northwest and is currently expanding its range westward. The two hybridize where their ranges overlap in the Great Plains, though the male Baltimore has a full black hood and much less white in his wings than the male Bullock's.

Year-round | Adult male

PURPLE FINCH

Carpodacus purpureus L 6" (15 cm)

FIELD MARKS

Adult male is not purple, but rose-red over body and brightest on head and rump

Females are brown and heavily streaked below on whitish belly

Strongly notched tail; stubby triangular bill

Behavior

Forages on ground and in trees primarily for seeds. Also consumes some insects, caterpillars, and fruits, particularly in summer. Seen singly or in a pair during breeding season, but will join mixed-species foraging flocks of siskins and goldfinches in winter. Male sings a rich warble from an exposed perch, sometimes incorporating the songs of other species. Calls include a musical *chur-lee* and, in flight, a sharp *pit*.

Habitat

Found in woodland edges, suburbs, parks, and orchards. Nests in the fork of a tree.

Local Sites

A permanent resident in the western portion of Washington and Oregon, look for the Purple Finch in the foothills of the Cascades and of Coast Ranges.

FIELD NOTES The similarly plumaged Cassin's Finch, *Carpodacus cassinii* (inset: male, left; female, right), can be quite a challenge to differentiate from the Purple Finch. The male is considerably browner on the back and does not show red on the underparts as extensively as the Purple. The female shows crisper streaking on her breast and, unlike the female Purple, has streaked undertail coverts. Both give a distinctive flight call, a high-pitched *kee-up*.

Year-round | Adult male

HOUSE FINCH

Carpodacus mexicanus L 6" (15 cm)

FIELD MARKS

Male's forehead, bib, and rump typically red, but can be orange or, occasionally, yellow

Brown streaked back; white belly; streaked flanks

Female streaked dusky brown on entire body

Behavior

A seed eater, the House Finch forages on the ground, in fields and in suburban yards. Often visits backyard feeders. Seen in large flocks during winter. Flies in undulating pattern, during which squared-off tail is evident. Male sings a conspicuously lively, high-pitched song consisting of varied three-note phrases, usually ending in a nasal *wheer*. Calls include a whistled *wheat*.

Habitat

Adaptable to varied habitats, this abundant bird prefers open areas, including suburban parks and areas where it can build its cup-like nest on buildings. Also nests in shrubs, trees, or on the ground.

Local Sites

A widespread bird, it can be found in any number of urban, suburban, or agricultural areas throughout much of Washington and Oregon.

FIELD NOTES The female House Finch (inset) is grayish brown overall and heavily streaked on her entire body. Pairs can often be found during breeding season, and small family groups after nesting, but this gregarious bird forms large foraging flocks for the winter, sometimes with other species of finches.

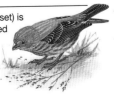

Year-round | Adult

PINE SISKIN

Carduelis pinus L 5" (13 cm)

FIELD MARKS

Streaked brown overall; short tail

Flight feathers and tail are washed with yellow, more evident on male

Two wing bars

Thin, pointed bill

Behavior

Almost always seen in flocks, foraging on the ground or in trees for seeds and, in summer, some insects. Often found in fields of thistle in the company of goldfinches. May also drink sap from tree wells drilled by sapsuckers. A highly nomadic species. Song is a twittering, variably pitched, jumbled warble. Call is an ascending, buzzy *zreee*. Flight call is a hoarse, repeated *chee*.

Habitat

Found mostly in coniferous or mixed woodlands. Erratic, unpredictable movement of flocks brings these birds also into urban parks and weedy fields. Will visit goldfinch feeders. Nest generally located far out on a branch of a conifer.

Local Sites

Siskins breed in the coniferous forests of all of Washington and Oregon's mountain ranges. In winter, they will descend to nearby foothills and valleys.

FIELD NOTES Another permanent resident of montane, coniferous forests in Washington and Oregon is the Red Crossbill, *Loxia curvirostra* (inset: female, top; male, bottom). Easily distinguished from siskins by overall body color, crossbills are distinctive in that their mandibles cross at the tips, enabling these birds to extract seeds with ease from the cones of coniferous trees.

Breeding | Adult male

AMERICAN GOLDFINCH

Carduelis tristis L 5" (13 cm)

FIELD MARKS
Breeding male bright yellow with black cap; female and winter male duller overall, lacking cap

Black wings with white wing bars

Black-and-white tail; white undertail coverts

Behavior
Gregarious and active. Winter flocks may contain a hundred or more goldfinches and include several other species. While it will sometimes eat insects as well, the typical goldfinch diet—mostly seeds— is the most vegetarian of any North American bird. During courtship, male performs exaggerated, undulating aerial maneuvers, and often feeds the incubating female. Song is a lively series of trills, twitters, and *swee* notes. Distinctive flight call is *per-chik-o-ree.*

Habitat
Found in weedy fields, open woodlands, and anywhere rich in thistles and sunflowers. Nests at forest edges or in old fields, often late in summer after thistles have bloomed so that the plant can be used as nest lining.

Local Sites
The state bird of Washington, the American Goldfinch is found in open areas throughout the region, except in higher elevations of the Cascade Range.

FIELD NOTES The slightly smaller Lesser Goldfinch, *Carduelis psaltria* (inset: female), reaches the northern limit of its range in the valleys and foothills of western Oregon. The male has a black cap, olive-green upperparts, black wings and tail, and bright yellow underparts. The female is similar, but lacks the black cap.

Year-round | Adult male

EVENING GROSBEAK

Coccothraustes vespertinus L 8" (20 cm)

FIELD MARKS
Stocky finch with large, pale yellow or greenish bill

Yellow eyebrow and forehead on adult male; dark brown and yellow body; white secondaries

Gray and tan female has thin, dark malar stripe; white-tipped tail

Behavior
Forages mostly in trees and shrubs for seeds, berries, and insects, sometimes searching on the ground. Also feeds on buds of deciduous trees, and maple sap. At bird feeders, the Evening Grosbeak is fond of sunflower seeds, and uses its powerful jaws to crack them open easily. Gregarious year-round, they travel in flocks and even build their nests near each other. Loud, strident calls include a *clee-ip* and a *peeer*. Song consists of regularly repeated call notes.

Habitat
Breeds in montane coniferous and mixed woods. In winter, descends to lower-elevation woodlots, shade trees, and feeders. Nest is usually far out on a horizontal branch of a tree.

Local Sites
Evening Grosbeaks can be found in summer in conifer forests in any of Washington and Oregon's mountain ranges, particularly Mt. Rainier in Washington.

FIELD NOTES A common visitor to backyard feeders, especially in winter, the Evening Grosbeak's pattern of occurrence may even be affected by the location and abundance of feeders. Grosbeaks may appear in one area one winter and be absent the next, perhaps because there is no need to roam much farther than the nearest accessible refueling station.

Breeding | Adult male

HOUSE SPARROW

Passer domesticus L 6¼" (16 cm)

FIELD MARKS

Breeding male has black bill, bib, and lores; chestnut eye stripes, nape, back, and shoulders

Winter male less patterned

Female has brown back, streaked with black; buffy eyestripe; and unstreaked grayish breast

Behavior

Abundant and gregarious year-round. Hops around, feeding on grain, seeds, and shoots, or seeks out bird feeders for sunflower seeds and millet. In urban areas, begs for food from humans and will clean up any crumbs left behind. In spring and summer, multiple male suitors will chase a possible mate in aerial pursuit. Females choose mate mostly according to song display. Singing males give persistent *cheep*.

Habitat

Found in close proximity to humans. Can be observed in urban and suburban areas and in rural landscapes inhabited by humans and livestock. Nests in any sheltered cavity, often usurping it from other species.

Local Sites

Abundant wherever humans habitate, House Sparrows flock in the most heavily urbanized areas.

FIELD NOTES Also known as the English Sparrow, the House Sparrow was first introduced into North America at New York's Central Park in the 1850s, in an effort to populate the park with all the birds mentioned in Shakespeare's plays. It has since spread across the continent to become one of the most successful bird species in North America, to the detriment of many native species. Ironically, its numbers are declining precipitously in its native England.

American Kestrel, 77

 Whimbrel, 89

 Wilson's Snipe, 95

 Mourning Dove, 115

 Barn Owl, 117

 Great Horned Owl, 119

 Common Nighthawk, 121

 Northern Flicker, 135

 Horned Lark, 161

 Say's Phoebe, 143

 Cliff Swallow, 165

 Brown Creeper, 179

 Bewick's Wren, 181

 House Wren, 183

 Winter Wren, 185

 Swainson's Thrush, 197

 Cedar Waxwing, 205

 Fox Sparrow, 225

Song Sparrow, 227

 Golden-crowned Sparrow, 229

 Pine Siskin, 255

 House Sparrow, 261

Mostly Brown and White

 Canada Goose, 19

 Northern Pintail, 33

 Osprey, 69

 Bald Eagle, 71

 Red-tailed Hawk, 75

 Killdeer, 81

 Spotted Sandpiper, 87

 Dunlin, 91

 Chipping Sparrow, 223

 White-crowned Sparrow, 231

Mostly Gray

 Great Blue Heron, 61

 Green Heron, 65

 Sanderling, 91

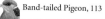

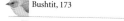

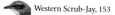

The main entry page number for each species is listed in **boldface** type and refers to the text page opposite the illustration.

A check-off box is provided next to each common-name entry so that you can use this index as a checklist of the species you have identified.

ACKNOWLEDGMENTS

The Book Division would like to thank the following people for their guidance and contribution in creating the *National Geographic Field Guide to Birds: Washington and Oregon*

Tom Vezo:

Tom Vezo is an award-winning wildlife photographer who is widely published throughout the U.S. and Europe. He specializes in bird photography but photographs other wildlife and nature subjects as well. He is a contributor to the *National Geographic Reference Atlas to the Birds of North America*. Please visit Tom at his website www.tomvezo.com.

Richard Crossley

Richard Crossley is an Englishman obsessed by birding since age 10. He traveled the world studying birds but fell in love with Cape May while pioneering the identification of overhead warbler migration in 1985. He is co-author of *The Shorebird Guide* due in Spring 2006.

Brian Sullivan:

Birding travels and field projects have taken Brian Sullivan to Central and South America, to the Arctic and across North America during the past 12 years. He has written and consulted on various books, and on popular, and scientific literature on North American birds. Research interests include migration, seabirds, raptors and bird identification. He is currently a PRBO Field Coordinator for the endangered San Clemente Loggerhead Shrike Recovery Project.

Brian E. Small:

Brian E. Small has been a full-time professional wildlife photographer specializing in birds for more than 15 years. In addition, he has been a regular columnist and Advisory Board member for *WildBird* magazine for the past 10 years. An avid naturalist and enthusiastic birder, Brian is currently the Photo Editor for the American Birding Association's *Birding* magazine. You can find more of his images at www.briansmallphoto.com.

Larry Sansone:

An active birder since 1960, Larry Sansone began photographing wildlife in the early 1970s. His pictures are published in field guides and magazines in the U.S. and Europe. He was a technical advisor to the first edition of the *National Geographic Field Guide to the Birds of North America*, and he is photo editor of *Rare Birds of California* by the California Bird Records Committee.

Cortez C. Austin, Jr.: pp. 20, 44, 82, 166; Richard Crossley: pp. 2, 40, 88, 198, 204; Mike Danzenbaker: pp. 122, 184; G.C. Kelley: p. 118; Gary Rosenberg: p. 250; Larry Sansone: pp. 48, 56, 96, 106, 112, 132, 138, 158, 162, 206, 212, 228, 236; Brian E. Small: pp. 14, 16, 36, 58, 66, 68, 76, 90, 92, 94, 100, 110, 114, 124, 128, 130, 134, 136, 140, 142, 144, 146, 148, 150, 152, 154, 160, 172, 178, 186, 192, 194, 196, 200, 210, 214, 216, 218, 220, 222, 224, 226, 232, 240, 242, 244, 248, 258; Tom Ulrich/Vireo:pp 170; Tom Vezo: cover, pp. 18, 22, 24, 26, 28, 30, 32, 34, 38, 42, 46, 50, 52, 54, 60, 62, 64, 70, 72, 74, 78, 80, 84, 86, 98, 102, 104, 108, 116, 120, 126, 156, 164, 168, 174, 176, 180, 182, 188, 190, 202, 208, 230, 234, 238, 246, 252, 254, 256, 260

NATIONAL GEOGRAPHIC
FIELD GUIDE TO BIRDS:
WASHINGTON & OREGON

Edited by Jonathan Alderfer

**Published by
the National Geographic Society**

John M. Fahey, Jr.,
President and Chief Executive Officer

Gilbert M. Grosvenor,
Chairman of the Board

Nina D. Hoffman,
Executive Vice President

Prepared by the Book Division

Kevin Mulroy,
Senior Vice President and Publisher

Kristin Hanneman, *Illustrations Director*

Marianne R. Koszorus, *Design Director*

Rebecca Hinds, *Managing Editor*

Carl Mehler, *Director of Maps*

Barbara Brownell Grogan,
Executive Editor

Staff for this Book

Kate Griffin, *Project Manager*

Dan O'Toole, *Writer, Illustrations Editor*

Alexandra Littlehales, *Designer*

Carol Norton, *Series Art Director*

Suzanne Poole, *Text Editor*

Teresa Neva Tate, *Illustrations Specialist*

Alan Conteras, Charlie Wright, Hendrik
Herlyn, *Map Research*

Matt Chwastyk, Sven Dolling,
Map Production

Lauren Pruneski, *Editorial Assistant*

Rick Wain, *Production Project Manager*

Manufacturing and Quality Control

Christopher A. Liedel,
Chief Financial Officer

Phillip L. Schlosser, *Managing Director*

John T. Dunn, *Technical Diurector*

Founded in 1888, the National
Geographic Society is one of the largest
nonprofit scientific and educational
organizations in the world. It reaches
more than 285 million people worldwide
each month through its official journal,
NATIONAL GEOGRAPHIC, and its four other
magazines; the National Geographic
Channel; television documentaries; radio
programs; films; books; videos and
DVDs; maps; and interactive media.
National Geographic has funded more
than 8,000 scientific research projects
and supports an education program
combating geographic illiteracy.

For more information, please call
1-800-NGS LINE (647-5463) or write
to the following address:

National Geographic Society
1145 17th Street N.W.
Washington, D.C. 20036-4688 U.S.A.

Log on to nationalgeographic.com;
AOL Keyword: NatGeo.

**Library of Congress
Cataloging-in-Publication Data**

Available upon request.
ISBN 0-7922-5313-2